THE LURE
OF
POKÉMON

THE LURE OF POKÉMON

Video Games and the Savage Mind

NAKAZAWA Shinichi

Japan Publishing Industry Foundation for Culture

A Note on Romanization

In the text of this book, the Hepburn system of romanization is used for Japanese terms, including the names of persons and places. Long vowels in Japanese words are represented by macrons (bars over vowels), except in well-known place names and words fully acculturated in the English language. Japanese names are given in Western order: personal name first, surname last, except on the jacket, cover, and title page where the name of the author is given in traditional order as Nakazawa Shinichi.

The Lure of Pokémon: Video Games and the Savage Mind
By Shinichi Nakazawa. Translated by Ted Mack.

Published by
Japan Publishing Industry Foundation for Culture (JPIC)
3-12-3 Kanda-Jinbocho, Chiyoda-ku, Tokyo 101-0051, Japan

First English edition: March 2019

Originally published in Japanese under the title *Poketto no naka no yasei* by Iwanami Shoten, Publishers in 1997, and republished in pocket paperback by Shinchosha Publishing Co., Ltd. in 2004 and in another pocket paperback format under the new title *Pokemon no shinwa gaku: Shinpan poketto no naka no yasei* by KADOKAWA CORPORATION in 2016.
English publishing rights arranged with KADOKAWA CORPORATION, Tokyo.

Jacket and cover design: Kazuhiko Miki, Ampersand Works
Jacket and cover illustration: © 1995 Nintendo / Creatures Inc. / GAME FREAK inc.

Printed in Japan
ISBN 978-4-86658-065-4
http://www.jpic.or.jp/japanlibrary/

Preface to the 2016 Edition

This book on *Pokémon* was first published in 1997 under the title *Poketto no naka no yasei* [The Wildness in Your Pocket]. The game *Pokémon*, originally *Pocket Monsters*, was released in February 1996 for Nintendo's portable Game Boy device. It did not have the 3D graphics it does now, but was a calm game of its time, with simple images, digitized music, and rudimentary animation. The game quickly became popular among primary school students, and it captured my attention too, to the point that I even decided to write books like this one about it. That was the summer of 1997, soon after the collapse of the bubble economy, when Japanese society was experiencing a spreading sense of hopelessness.

I became attracted to *Pokémon* when I discovered that the game provided a vibrant and generous venue for the exercise of something that had seemed to have disappeared from contemporary society: the "savage mind." The pocket monsters were superb (and adorable) models of that power, which wells up from the unconscious. I was also captivated by the brilliant device of the "Poké Balls," which let you capture Pokémon and make them your own.

The world of *Pokémon* is built from the very elemental thought at which the ancients so excelled. It overflows with the passion for creative categorization that primitive societies value; we see this passion expressed even in the nature of the battles, through which power is exchanged. Put simply, the game *Pokémon* brims with the mythic elements that arouse my imagination as an anthropologist.

Time passed and this book, after coming out in paperback, went out of print. Lately it is hard to even find a copy. My cute Pokémon live a life of peaceful seclusion, all cozy inside the Game Boy on the corner of my desk—except for the rare occasion when I rouse them like an old memory.

This past summer, however, a big event rocked the peaceful

Pokémon world. The app *Pokémon GO* was released and quickly swept the globe. Those pocket monsters began appearing on the screens of smartphones, this time against real-world backgrounds, and crowds of people trying to catch them swarmed the streets from early morning until late at night. Old fans who have played the game since its inception and newcomers who had never heard of it became obsessed with *Pokémon GO* and scenes of them tracking down the little monsters were played out again and again.

When this "*Pokémon* Rhapsody" swept over the world, I received emails and phone calls from a number of people saying with great excitement that "the very thing you described in that book happened to me!" At the beginning of the book, there is a scene in which a group of children are playing *Pokémon* on a device in one hand even as they catch tadpoles and crayfish with the other. When I first saw that, I felt as though I had been granted a glimpse of humankind moving into the future. Today, some twenty years later, that scene is playing out before my eyes again, this time using the most advanced AR (Augmented Reality) technology—and on a global scale. It struck me as uncanny.

I downloaded *Pokémon GO* right away and set out into the night streets. Despite the late hour, people holding smartphones were amassed in city parks, milling around in search of Pokémon. It was a bizarre sight. Notwithstanding occasional problems with littering, noise, and other disturbances, for the most part the members of these crowds struck me as good people. People who probably worked hard at their jobs and in their homes during the day. People assimilated into human society who, when night falls, secretly gather in nearby parks to make merry—not by holding a dance as in a fairy tale, but by searching for Pokémon. Thinking about this made me chuckle.

Coming back into contact with the Pokémon I had once held dear inspired a variety of thoughts. What I wrote in this book leaves out a great deal. I had a strong urge to write a new book on *Pokémon* that included *Pokémon GO*.

As the father of the game, Satoshi Tajiri, wrote in his afterword to this volume, in 1997 *Pokémon* was approaching a watershed moment. The game was booming, but at the same time there were rumors of an animated show, and the *Pokémon* cards that had spun off from the game were selling wildly. An uncontrollable force was changing *Pokémon* itself, and sending it toward a more expansive future. This was the exciting presentiment that was spreading through society. In my next book, I hope to write about the monstrous form these little creatures took when they became a megahit commodity beloved the world over. At the same time, though, I have recently begun to feel that the essence of *Pokémon* has not changed that much after all. Even in this *Pokémon* world that has spread across the globe and become increasingly complex, there seems to be a "*Pokémon* principle" that survives unchanged, regardless of the country, region, or time.

When you think about it, the seeds for the evolution to *Pokémon GO* were already sown in the original *Pokémon*. Whether that evolution will be for the better or for the worse is yet to be seen. However, as long as the games are created, as Tajiri says, from the "real drives of children," *Pokémon*'s development is unlikely to run astray. I look forward to seeing how these little monsters born of the depths of Japanese culture will weather the world, not just Japan, in the twenty-first century.

Shinichi Nakazawa
August 2016
Tokyo

CONTENTS

"But, whether one deplores or rejoices in the fact, there are still zones in which savage thought, like savage species, is relatively protected. This is the case of art, to which our civilization accords the status of a national park, with all the advantages and inconveniences attending so artificial a formula; and it is particularly the case of so many as yet 'uncleared' sectors of social life, where, through indifference or inability, and most often without our knowing why, primitive thought continues to flourish."

Claude Lévi-Strauss, *The Savage Mind*, trans. John and Doreen Weightman (London: Weidenfeld and Nicolson, 1966), p. 219.

Prologue

There are always new discoveries to make when one talks with game designers. These men and women labor as if directly touching the unconscious minds of children and the young at heart. It closely resembles the way a ceramicist works clay. But what game designers mold is the pliantly changing unconscious, which they knead until it becomes one dynamic mass. Seeing them at work, I feel as though I have become a psychiatrist deftly applying sandplay therapy, holding my breath as I watch an elaborate, miniature world of the unconscious take shape before my eyes. At such moments, I am filled with excitement.

This is precisely how I felt when I spoke with the designer of *Pokémon* (Pocket Monsters), Satoshi Tajiri. What made me want to meet and speak with him so much was the number of times I had come across scenes like this: one Sunday after the game had become tremendously popular, mostly among children in the lower grades of primary school, I happened to be walking along the Tama River when I noticed a number of children caught up in trying to catch tadpoles and crayfish in pools along its banks. That in and of itself would not be noteworthy, but what caught my attention was the fact that among those children I could see some who held small game devices in their free hands. I asked my young friend, who knew a lot about games, what it was they were playing. In response, he answered casually, "Oh, that? They are playing *Pokémon*. Playing *Pokémon* while fishing... Now that's a cutting-edge scene, isn't it?"

Not quite understanding what he meant by "cutting-edge," I asked him to elaborate. He explained that it was an RPG (role-playing game) in which players capture wild monsters that are hidden in places like forests, fields, and caves, and then raise and train them to fight opponents, with the ultimate goal of collecting all of the 151 types that inhabit the "game universe." In other words, these children are working diligently to capture a kind of "life" as they move back and forth between two different types of spaces: one in which they collect imaginary monsters who live behind the small, liquid crystal displays of their game devices, and the other in which they catch and play with fish and bugs and other creatures in real ponds.

Children who fish as they play *Pokémon* seem to be trying to create a type of passage between things created by nature and the pseudo-nature created by technology. For the most part, Japanese people have a tendency not to see nature and technology in opposition in the way that Westerners do. Technology is seen not as something that suppresses or destroys nature, but rather as a tool for drawing out what might be called "the essence of nature," which lies hidden within it. The Japanese built their civilization enveloped by rich nature. With the arrival of the West, Japanese civilization and nature alike have rapidly changed as new science and technology have flowed into the country. During this process, the Japanese have sought to customize these technologies to truly enrich their spirits and lives. Japanese tradition already attests to the fact that technology need not oppose nature but can be used together with it to maximize the potential of both. Once this is achieved, the future of the Japanese opens up before them. These were the thoughts that came to me when I saw children carrying both crayfish and small game devices with *Pokémon* on them.

Some days later I had a chance to meet and speak with Satoshi Tajiri. With all the things I wanted to ask him, it was a deeply one-sided interview. Tajiri, for his part, never showed any frustration and answered each of my questions thoughtfully.

Nakazawa: Tell me about your childhood, before you got involved with games. You were born in 1965, correct?

Tajiri: That's right. I grew up in Machida. At the time, Machida was a part of the Tokyo metropolitan area in name only; it was still a quite undeveloped suburb, with large rice paddies and forests. I enjoyed catching insects in those paddies and forests and keeping crayfish as pets. I was the type of kid who became obsessed with things; I dreamed up various methods of catching insects more effectively than those the other kids were using.

Nakazawa: For example?

Tajiri: Most children left out honey to attract insects, but I thought of the idea of leaving rocks at the roots of trees. I had noticed that the insects that were active at night came down from the trees and slept hidden beneath rocks. In addition to techniques for capturing insects, I also did a lot of research into ways to help them live longer. For example, when keeping insects through the winter, it is better to keep them in a slightly cold place rather than a warm one. When the temperature variation throughout the day is smaller, the insects move less and live longer. I put experiences such as these to use in designing *Pokémon*. Many of the ideas that form the basis for *Pokémon* come from the world I lived in during my primary school days.

Nakazawa: But wasn't it during your middle school years that *Space Invaders* came out and revolutionized the lives of children?

Tajiri: I will never forget it. It was when we were in our first year of middle school. *Space Invaders* just appeared one day. It was a real shock. Things really turned upside down from that day on; it was stunning. I couldn't believe my eyes when I saw the *Space Invaders* machines lined up in the rooftop arcade of our suburban department store, which had been filled with pinball machines to that point. It took no time at all for me to become completely obsessed with it. Throughout middle school and high school, all I did was play these games; without me even realizing, my intense experience of nature from my primary school days went dormant for some time after the appearance of *Space Invaders.*

Nakazawa: Would you say that there was a drastic discontinuity between your experiences with catching insects and your experiences with video games?

Tajiri: Simply calling it a discontinuity doesn't seem to quite get it, I think. There was some continuity . . . Suffice to say that many dramatic changes were occurring simultaneously around that time. Machida, where I lived, was changing rapidly as open fields disappeared with the area's urbanization. Rice paddies and forests were being developed, and houses were being built everywhere. I completely forgot about insects and devoted myself to video games.

......

Nakazawa: But those intense experiences of collecting insects during your primary school days, which were dormant during that period, really came back in *Pokémon*, didn't they? Albeit in a different form.

Tajiri: That's right. When I was designing the game, I tried very hard to remember how I had thought when I myself was a child. In so doing, a lot of long-forgotten memories came back to me. For example, the idea for the water type Pokémon "Poliwag" came directly from the polliwogs I had seen in the rice paddies of Machida. When I was in primary school, I had often scooped them up and observed them closely. I remember staring at their intestines, which are visible through their transparent bodies. I was really fascinated by that. I came up with a lot of the monsters this way.

Nakazawa: There are lots of caves in the game. In American games, caves are dungeons that seem to represent the world of the dead; by contrast, in *Pokémon*, even when they resemble these dungeons, caves feel more like storehouses of life, and we feel a certain affection for them.

Tajiri: In terms of caves and dungeons, when we were children, we often played in the developed areas of Machida. There were a lot of places where holes had been dug for drainage canals, but not completed and just left unfinished and unused. We used to explore those places. Going into these dark holes, we would emerge suddenly at rivers and so on. In designing the game, we were trying to recreate these places that we had experienced as children.

Nakazawa: The world that the children who are obsessed with *Pokémon* live in today is quite different from this. Instead of becoming obsessed with catching insects, they are forced to study constantly, and rice paddies and forests have all but disappeared. What they become obsessed with is *Pokémon*. It's an interesting phenomenon.

Tajiri: I often think about this too. I don't believe that what children are interested in, what children really want, changes from generation to generation. I think there are things they don't do because their environments don't happen to allow it, but what they want is still the same. Don't you think that, coming across some cave, a child today would still imagine it to be a dungeon and be overcome with the impulse to explore it? If you intentionally make for them something that used to be but no longer is, I think they will happily play with it. We just happened to live in an environment that allowed us to realize those desires. Children today have the same desires, but, because of their environments, those desires cannot simply emerge. The children who are obsessed with *Pokémon* are primarily third- and fourth-graders, which is around the age that kids begin to ride bicycles. It is a time when the area in which they can roam grows suddenly, which stimulates their imaginations and activities. It is a time when they sense the expansion of their worlds. When we were creating *Pokémon*, we did ask ourselves whether children today, who do not come into contact with much nature, would enjoy the game, but that concern was unnecessary. This is why I suspect that children's fundamental desires do not change with time or depending on the worlds they live in.

(Unpublished discussion held at Game Freak with Satoshi Tajiri, 5 March 1997)

What Tajiri refers to as the fundamental desires of children, which do not change with time or depend on the world in which they live, are none other than Claude Lévi-Strauss's "savage mind." The savage mind is not something possessed by primitive societies alone. It is alive and well in the contemporary world as well. Sometimes it even flourishes to the point of attracting the disapproval of the "serious adults" of that world. Video games are a case in point. The video game *Pokémon* succeeded in giving these impulses that abide in the unconscious minds of children straightforward and rich expression. At this moment, these children's desires take the form of the savage mind.

Immediately we can imagine the voices of criticism from mothers and teachers all around us who tell children to "quit playing games all the time and get back to your studies!" In a tiny device of about 3 x 5 inches, however, the game artificially creates a territory in which the contemporary savage mind, like areas of wild flora and fauna, is relatively well protected. Needless to say, it does not receive the same sympathetic treatment as a national park; you could even say that it is under constant threat. In fact, many of the children who are currently obsessed with the game will, after some years, naturally leave this protected area of the savage mind, ultimately even forgetting why they were so obsessed with that world in the first place.

Even if these children do forget, however, the savage mind is unlikely to be eliminated from the human race. There are always adults like Tajiri, who think about their childhoods and attempt to pass on to the next generation a "tradition" or type of "genetic information" that gives shape to those unconscious desires in a way that is faithful to their memories of what they felt as children. This gives the savage mind a new shape for a different environment and a different generation.

In this book, I attempt to travel though the caves and fields and forests of this game world like a sort of wild animal reserve ranger, observing every nook and cranny of this biome of savage mind that still flourishes in the lives of contemporary Japanese children, and produce a manual for its protection.

CHAPTER 1

THE *SPACE INVADERS* REVOLUTION

T he world of video games has already developed into quite a complex one. This makes it extremely difficult to clarify the relationship between those games and children's unconscious minds. The best approach in such a situation is to go back to the beginning. The most salient beginning in this case is *Space Invaders*.

Space Invaders was first released in Japan in 1978 and precipitated a massive change in the world of children's games. Looking back, the game is quite simplistic, but there was more to it than initially met the eye. When we think structurally about the many games that followed, most of them can be thought of as variations of *Space Invaders* and its formidable simplicity. The game presents the essence of video games in an almost completely unadorned form.

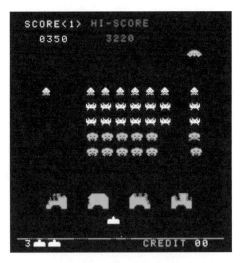

***Space Invaders* gameplay**
(Courtesy of Taito Corporation)

Small, white masses of light appear suddenly from the black space of the screen. These are the enemy invaders, which assemble and march in a strict formation until (in later manifestations of the game) they split apart and curve off in various directions. The player fires upon these points of light. Once struck, the aliens burst into droplets of light and disappear, absorbed once again into the pitch-black space. The game consists merely of a repetition of these simple actions.

To my mind, the key point here is the ease with which these masses of light appear and disappear. Named "invaders," they emerge suddenly from the darkness. We have no idea where they come from. Moreover, they just keep coming. Made entirely of light, these invaders give us none of the characteristic sense of resistance that materiality would provide. As if merely enjoying the lightness of being, they waft into view, float lightly from side to side, and then disappear as if extinguished.

The first time I saw the game, it struck me that they looked just like elementary particles. Elementary particles appear one after another from "fields" of amassed wave energy, existing for the briefest of moments before they disappear once more into the latent field. The invaders appear in a remarkably similar way.

Back when computer graphics were not as sophisticated as they are now, the simple, pitch-black screen seemed just like an energy field that spawned the invaders. It behaved not like an empty void, but rather a latent field, filled with energy, that produced and then extinguished masses of light in the form of disks and rockets. Energy, granted the nearly weightless materiality of light, sprang forth into this world. During their brief existence on the screen, these masses formed ranks, changed the direction of their movement, and were beset upon by similarly weightless attacks launched by the player, upon which they vanished into the black space again like the most delicate and fragile of objects. That the invaders continued to appear, one after another, was precisely the attraction of the game.

Space Invaders presented this new space, never seen before, to children. Thanks to developments in technology, the computer monitor became a nothingness filled with hidden energy that brought forth curious bodies of light that could be neither given meaning nor situated within any existing system and then suddenly extinguished them, one after another. In no time at all children were enthralled.

Why? I think it was because children had always had such a space in their minds and were always unconsciously perceiving what went on there. It surprised and delighted them to see their psychic processes brought out before their eyes in such an impressive way. When Satoshi Tajiri spoke (in the interview that appears in this volume) of the "impact of the appearance of *Space Invaders*," this is what he meant.

What the appearance of real video games showed children was their own unconscious minds. The "interaction" between children and games began there. Players faced these "invaders" on-screen, launching various attacks against them that appeared to extinguish these masses of light instantly. These disappearances produced immediate effects in the unconscious. As these codes made up only of light appeared and disappeared, the process passed through the child's eyes and into his mind, triggering a similar process within his unconscious that produced an internal sense of pleasure from the game.

So, just what is happening at this moment inside the child's unconscious mind? Surprisingly, Freud has already given us a near-complete answer to this question. His famous writings about the *Fort/Da* (Gone/There) game are hugely important to understanding the essence of today's video games.

Later in his life, Freud was asked by his daughter to watch her one-and-a-half-year-old son. One day he noticed that the boy, who was still developing the ability to speak, was doing something unusual. Freud had thought that the boy was merely fiddling with one of the spools of thread that his mother used in her work, until the boy yelled "*Fort!*" (Gone!) and threw the spool away. He then grabbed the end of the thread that had come unwound from the spool, yelled "*Da!*" (There!), and pulled the spool back to himself, beaming with satisfaction. Freud thought that would be the end of it, but the boy then threw the spool away again with another cry of "*Fort!*" Time and again he repeated the sequence exactly.

Freud watched this process carefully, trying to ascertain the meaning of the boy's actions. At that time, Freud was intensely preoccupied with the concept he would later come to refer to as the "death drive." Freud's theory was that as well as the desire that drove humans toward life, Eros, there was another, hidden impulse that compelled them toward death, Thanatos. If such a drive did not exist, humans' ability to enjoy uncanny experiences and frightening stories would be unfathomable, as would their eagerness to injure and destroy themselves and others. Freud was on the verge of a revolutionary idea, and here with his grandson he finally discovered it; the endlessly repeated *Fort/Da* game, he surmised, might clearly reveal the existence of this "death drive" hidden within humankind.

Freud's interpretation was as follows: the boy was keenly affected by his mother's absence from the home, leaving him feeling anxious. Bereft of that kind person who was always by his side to protect him, the boy reached out for a nearby object: the spool that his mother was always using. By throwing the spool away from himself, he was symbolically representing his own plight: "My mother is gone!" Perhaps at some level he was trying to grasp the irresolvable and distressing situation into which he had been placed symbolically, through fantasy, by using his own power to throw the spool as far away as possible and then bring it back again.

Gone! There! Gone! There!

The child attempts, through the power of symbols, to change a situation over which he is powerless into one that he can control. This act of symbolization is a form of magic that no one had to teach him, by which he attempts to alter reality itself and bring his absent mother back. This, however, leaves one thing unexplained. If casting away and reeling back the spool is a way of symbolically surmounting the anxiety of his mother's absence, why does he repeat the action over and over? An infant maintains its sense of self through identification with its mother. The mere absence of the boy's mother must produce an anxiety powerful enough to threaten his very existence. So why does the child intentionally and repeatedly cast the spool away to arouse this feeling?

Freud's theory was that the human mind harbors an attraction to the anxieties and fears that threaten its existence. From the depths of the unconscious, Thanatos, the death drive, urges humankind unrelentingly toward death and self-destruction. It is a drive to destroy the living individual and, in so doing, free oneself into the universal expanse of life unlimited. Eros presses back against this. Eros resists Thanatos's attempts to dissolve the individual into the universal "flow of life," working as a powerful desire to protect individual life as it is.

By the terms of this logic, the meaning of the child's "magic" with the spool is clear. The act of casting the spool away and then reeling it back has a double meaning. First, overlaying a symbolic system made up of ones (presence) and zeroes (absence) upon the anxiety welling up within him is the child's instinctive attempt to control that internal emotional chaos. But once the child can do this, he becomes unable to suppress the urge to use those symbolic tools to approach the source of that anxiety and fear over and over again. That is to say, a human child is a curious creature, driven to recreate the circumstances that plunge him into anxiety so long as a mechanism exists for ensuring his symbolic safety.

The idea that Freud's "death drive" is related to this sort of magic or play that children engage in with such innocence has the ring of truth. This is clear in the case of *Space Invaders*. In the *Fort/Da* game, the appearance and subsequent disappearance of the spool create a simple symbolic system. That system, by being applied directly to the anxiety that wells up from within the child, prevents that emotion from invading the child's mind in its raw form. In this way, the child is able to bear the anxiety. Having utilized these symbols, the child can engage in this play that allows him or her to voluntarily approach the source of that anxiety once again.

A similar process is at work in *Space Invaders*. Through the skillful manipulation of his controls, the player attacks the masses of light that appear upon the screen. If the player's aim is true, the aliens that are hit wink out of existence. One after another, they appear from the depths of the pitch-black monitor, then are sucked back into the pitch-black darkness the instant they come into contact with the player's consciousness. The "Gone/There" game is recreated. The video game produces the illusion that the screen is a thin boundary behind which exists a latent energy field that produces and then reabsorbs individuality.

Observing one's own psyche while absorbed in *Space Invaders*, one feels the game is making contact with the processes going on continuously in the depths of the mind, but doing so with a light touch. Shooting and destroying the invaders does not provoke the heavy emotions that accidentally injuring or killing a living creature would, as they are merely dots of light. They do not possess the stability of being that a living organism possessing individuality — a frog, dragonfly, or butterfly, for example — does. The invaders exist in a state between the real and the virtual, limited to an ambiguous, uncertain existence. This is why they appear and disappear with equal ease. The repetition of this sequence forms a thin membrane of symbols directed toward the rumbling of the "death drive." The game lets players touch and influence what is occurring at quite a deep level of life, where Eros and Thanatos interact freely.

Observing the spontaneous play of a child, Freud vividly perceived that it was taking place in the abyss of Thanatos. Were he alive to see today's flourishing video game industry, the prescience of his own insight might startle him. Digital technology succeeded in creating an easy-to-use method of interactively addressing the activities of the "death drive" that, in a child's mind, are still laid bare, not yet having been fully symbolized.

The appearance of this "interactive media" made activity in the depths of the mind, once the province of psychoanalysts and other specialists, readily accessible to everyone, whether in the arcade on the corner or on a home computer. *Space Invaders* was the starting point. It is the alpha and the omega of all the games that followed it, already starkly revealing every possibility within video games and every problematic aspect of their ability to affect children's psyches.

The felicitous name *Space Invaders* was crucial to its power. Naming those tiny characters made up of light "invaders" endowed the game with the capacity to invade deeply into its players' unconscious minds. There are any number of testimonies to this fact.

> ...*Space Invaders* is a good example. Most people probably remember that *Space Invaders* was popular back then, in 1979. If we expand our recollection a bit, we might also recall that *Star Wars* was made in 1977 and its sequel, *The Empire Strikes Back*, in 1980. People around the world were captivated with space as a result. In Japan, the film *Space Battleship Yamato* was released in 1977. I remember getting up at the crack of dawn to line up to see it. *Galaxy Express 999* was released in 1979, and Leiji Matsumoto's view of space became extremely popular, particularly among junior high school and high school fans of anime. *Space Invaders* appeared in 1978. As you can see, the timing of its release coincided with this boom. That point is that, at the time, people around the world shared a sense that something might exist up there. They say that *Space Invaders* was originally designed as a tank battle game, and then, just as the creators were beginning to worry that it was odd that the tanks moved side-to-side, *Star Wars* was released. It became a video game in

which players shoot invaders from space, rather than tanks, after the designers realized that there was nothing unusual about space invaders moving in any direction, and no ethical concern with shooting and killing them.

(Satoshi Tajiri, *New Game Design*, Enix, 1996: 26-27.)

Once the designers began to see the masses of light as invaders instead of tanks, an enormous change occurred. A game about tanks moving around on the ground, no matter how profound the interactions between player and game, could never descend to the "primal repression" (*Urverdrängung*) level of the unconscious, where the symbolic system comes into contact with the desire to destroy a living thing. When a tank is destroyed, it leaves wreckage on the ground. This "ground" upon which the game unfolds is already firmly incorporated within a stable sign system and cannot become a "field" from which some sort of being appears and disappears.

A tank battle also raises ethical questions. When someone present in this world is injured and killed, denied their existence, painful grief is felt. These sensations would also be triggered by a shooting game that targeted tanks moving across the surface of the earth. But the moment we reimagine that surface as the limitless expanse of space and those masses of light as vaguely defined "invaders" that cannot be situated within the context of our world, everything changes. The game swiftly and smoothly descends into the oceanic depths of the unconscious, just as the "Gone/There" game did, approaching the "primal repression" level where the "death drive" operates. Long before the astronauts of the Apollo missions reported their awe at the vastness of space, the word had already become synonymous with the mind in the popular imagination. "Space" was a vessel containing a boundless expanse and filled with the latent energy from which were created matter, life, and consciousness. When the monitor's pitch-black screen was presented as this sort of "space," it connected immediately and directly to the player's unconscious.

The invaders themselves were unidentified flying objects outside of any symbolic system, or perhaps representing a kind of "pre-symbolic" immediate predecessor to one. Even though they reflect the very boundary between the latent and the manifest, they do not fully exist in this world. They therefore function in common thought (though philosophers such as Emmanuel Lévinas would think differently) as structures that do not evoke the emotions behind ethics.

When the player shoots in the game, it does not signify the destruction of his opponent. The function of his shots is to push objects that have only barely emerged into the manifest (real) world back across the boundary into latent space. It is a prototype of violence that precedes violence. The shots repress the drive to destroy a living thing, to invade its interiority, forcing the impulse back across the boundary while maintaining an awareness of its existence. This was the profound change that the simple act of renaming the tanks "invaders" produced in video games.

CHAPTER 2.

THE BIRTH OF MONSTERS

T he "invaders" that appeared in front of children possessed characteristics that made them very similar to dreams. Among those, three of the most distinctive were:

1. Where they come from is unclear.
2. They appear, one after another, endlessly. That is, they are a multiplicity.
3. The process of their appearance and disappearance occurs smoothly.

They appear with no warning, slip away if you try to catch them, and then reappear just when you thought they had escaped. Despite these characteristics of unreliability and transience, they fascinate people and persistently stick with them thanks to a power that is hard to identify.

The French psychoanalyst Jacques Lacan referred to this hard-to-grasp phenomenon as the *objet petit a.*

The term *objet petit a* is used to refer to objects that appear in various forms at the periphery of consciousness and are very difficult to name.

The *objet petit a* is a remainder left behind from the world that has been symbolized using language. It is a strange thing, at once ambiguous, fragile, and not clearly consolidated as an object, but also difficult to bring under the complete control of the conscious mind and therefore ultimately of uncertain content and power. Above all, one cannot identify its origins. This is because it appears precisely on the boundary between things that can eventually be made conscious after being grasped through the power of language, and unconscious desires that cannot be symbolized through words, making its source impossible to express.

This is the reason that the *objet petit a* is fundamentally ambivalent, simultaneously belonging and not belonging to both self and other. One could say that the *objet petit a* bubbles up, again and again, from the periphery, or "edges," of consciousness, or from the fissures or "gaps" present in a world produced through the precisely organized system of language. The result is that it emerges as multiple things, all at once, and does so again and again. Their nature is also visible in the nature of their forms. The *objet petit a* has no fixed form, so whether one refers to it as amorphous or anomalous the point is that it possesses a surplus that causes it to exceed the senses and systems of the conscious mind.

Through the *objet petit a*, humans come into contact with life itself. At the boundary where life and the system of language meet, a primal repression is taking place. If the primal repression were not to function properly, this excess power, which cannot be controlled by language or symbolic systems, would flood the mind. Preventing this is the function of the primal repression at this boundary. When the power of life itself, which cannot be symbolized in the mind (itself a creation of the linguistic order), slips past this repression, it appears in the form of the *objet petit a*. Of course, it does not appear in the center of consciousness but on the periphery, on the "edges," "gaps," and "fissures," taking many forms to tempt us. This temptation has a particularly powerful effect on the minds of children, who find it extremely difficult to resist and easily fall under the spell of this *objet petit a* as it comes unrelentingly in a variety of different forms.

In the minds of children, their extreme interest in bodily discharge and the separation of things that were originally part of their bodies is always a significant issue. This has been understood through such concepts as Melanie Klein's "part-object." In the process of growing into an adult, the child must now distance herself from this once-vital part of herself in order to enter into the language of the symbolic father. Even once the child has grown into an adult, however, the *objet petit a* remains just visible at the edges and in the fissures of consciousness, casting quick glances at and whispering things to the "child" that still sleeps in the adult heart. When children come into contact with the representations of the *objet petit a* through sight, sound, taste, or touch, they experience pleasure at the sensation of having recovered the "remainders of symbolization" that they have been forced to repress, detach from, or discard in the process of growing into adults. It is as though they have come into contact with the living, breathing, pristine "nature" within themselves. When they interact with the *objet petit a* that appears as an image in their video game, they feel this raw, unconscious sensation within them through their eyes and ears and skin, just as previous generations of children were impressed when they saw the moving insides of transparent tadpoles, or caught bugs in a butterfly net and then grabbed them with their bare hands, or felt the movement in their wrists through fishing rods as a fish they had just landed thrashes in the water.

The *objet petit a* is constantly assuming different forms. It squirms and swarms its way into existence in multiple guises, uncontained by the symbolic order, coming into this world after the flow of excessive desire has been processed at the edges of consciousness. One thing it may do when it emerges is indicate a boundary through sheer multiplicity, even if, like the "invaders," its precise characteristics are unclear. This is the disruption of the senses that occurs simply as a result of scale, as when a herd of buffalo tears across a grassy field or a mass of protestors who have gathered in a public square begin to march. It is similar to the dizzying sensation one is liable to fall into when one sees newly laid frogspawn or stares at a mass of salmon roe on a dinner plate. *Space Invaders* possesses the power to rouse in the player this sort of strangely vivid sensation by producing a multitude of lights upon the screen, over and over again.

Another, different thing the manifestations of the *objet petit a* do through their diversity is reawaken people's sensitivity to the edges of consciousness. Excessive life force does not discover a "set place for itself" within the sensations or the symbolic order; rather, when it attempts to shape its own excess, diverse "monsters" appear. In contrast to the invaders, which lack individuality, these monsters exhibit excessive individuality when they appear ominously at the edges of our world as forms taken by the *objet petit a*. In this area too, Japanese culture in the 1970s displayed a surprising degree of development.

It goes without saying that *Ultraman* was the greatest achievement in this area. *Ultraman* realized a wealth of diversity that had not been seen in the world of monsters prior to that time. In other words, it skillfully shaped the *objet petit a* that appears on the edges of consciousness and surprised us with an infinite-seeming variety of forms. The only earlier creation that came close to this achievement were the *Illustrated Night Parade of One Hundred Demons* (*Hyakki yakō zu*) works, which were popular during the Edo period (1603–1868). Those masterpieces presented monsters in more than one hundred different forms—beneath bridges, under willow trees, beside the long walls surrounding warriors' mansions, in the woods around shrines, and in valleys deep in the mountains. In 1970s Japan, when progress was so thoroughly replacing darkness with brightly lit streets and eliminating those sources for monsters, *Ultraman* created new situations for the emergence of dramatically transformed manifestations of the *objet petit a*.

At that time, Japan was plagued with serious destruction and pollution of nature. The relationship between humans and nature was severely strained. The monsters that appear in *Ultraman* represented expressions of the power of nature, unleashed after this balance was lost. The monsters appeared on television in different guises each week. Humankind was at a loss as to how to control them. It was at this moment that Ultraman appeared.

Though Ultraman was an alien, he knew that there existed something pure in the hearts of earthlings, so he decided to help us. Because the monsters are manifestations of the *objet petit a* on a planetary scale, destroying them or driving them back into the depths of space was no simple task. Moreover, the monsters did not begin as enemies of humankind; rather, they are expressions of the now-warped power of nature, produced by an Earth that is out of balance. Ultraman battled these monsters on behalf of humankind, despite sympathizing with them.

The children watching this on television went wild for these unique monsters that appeared one after another. In the depths of their hearts, they sensed that they were manifestations of the very nature that humankind had mistreated, and therefore that they were also manifestations of the children themselves. They even felt sympathy for the monsters that were defeated by Ultraman, just as they had for Godzilla. Here we see an excellent example of the Japanese mind.

Alien Baltan (left) and Ultraman (right)
© TSUBURAYA PRODUCTIONS

Rather than repressing the urges that seep out from the edges of consciousness, the adults who created these monsters provided those desires with a pathway into the visible world by giving them ambiguous forms marked by change and instability. They did not deny the existence of edges or gaps in the world of science, or of the things that appear from these cracks in the system, but acknowledged that the system of language is not complete and provided appropriate interim shapes to the urges that slip through those fissures. The essence of this "Ultraman Project" was to suppress these invisible desires, as gently as the primal repression first used by the mind of an infant, by pulling them into the visible world.

I doubt there has ever been another group of people who have put such zeal into an endeavor like this. Here the secret of the Japanese mind's makeup is unintentionally put on display. The monsters, in constantly proliferating variety, are perpetually dispatched from the edges of consciousness. Each time the *objet petit a* metamorphizes, it appears before the children's eyes having scooped up new energy from the drives that exist prior to representation. The children cannot look away. The monsters, in their beguiling forms, dive into the children's unconscious minds, inhabiting the edges and gaps of consciousness they discover there. Thus, giant representations of the *objet petit a* are placed on the "edges" of consciousness. Formless urges are neither repressed nor liberated, but merely given shape. This is the secret of *Ultraman*, which in turn is directly connected to the secret of Japanese culture.

Put simply, this way of thinking is close to magic, because it also knowingly attempts to manage objects and phenomena not susceptible to logic. Magical thinking does not draw reasoned conclusions as science would, based on actual, quantifiable measurements of—for example—ozone concentration, barometric pressure, or changes in atmospheric carbon dioxide levels. Instead, it is interested in latent processes that occur behind, or at the deepest levels of, such measurable quantitative changes. Magical thinking concludes that the true root of what appears at the surface level to be degradation of the ozone layer is actually an imbalance in the relationship among the four classical elements of fire, earth, air, and water at the "molecular level" of that phenomenon.

Magic favors this way of thinking precisely because, contrary to how magic is normally understood, it lacks a belief in the omnipotence of language. Science attempts to express "truth" using the system of language. Science has faith that what is hidden in nature will, with sufficient human effort, eventually become expressible in words. Magic, however, doubts the omnipotence of language from the very start.

Magic has long thought of the system of language as a kind of incomplete net cast across the limitless depths and expanse of space. Language is always insufficient for that which takes place in space. Things exceed language. Emotion spills over the dam of language, and the mysteries of existence outstrip it by far. To make up for this insufficiency, magical thinking directs itself toward the border region that stretches out between things and words—the boundary at which language comes in contact with what has endless depth, and the reality of things confronts the systematicity of language in an almost threatening way. At that boundary region where the drives that well up from life change shape and become language, and latent power manifests in actual things, magic has made all things of this world into the objects of its thought.

Imagine the humans who lived in the verdant canyons of southern France roughly 30,000 years ago and painted animals on the walls of what would later be referred to as the Lascaux Cave. With only the light of a small oil lamp to guide them, they descended deeper and deeper into the caverns, groping along the rock walls. When they found a portion of the stone surface that was appropriate for painting, they took out their pigments and began to draw large elk on the wall using chisel-like tools of wood and rock. The faint lamplight would illuminate no more than ten centimeters in any direction. Little by little, the images of the elk, drawn with red and yellow pigments, would emerge on the rock. We might refer to what the people of Lascaux were doing back then as "magical arts."

Why magic? Because they thought that the artistic act that they were engaged in would manifest animals from a virtual space. In the interior of the earth, on the hidden rock walls deep within the cavern, these Paleolithic individuals perceived the actuality of the power of "fecund nature" in the form of mothers and women. Thanks to that power, vast herds of elk and bison would appear the following spring in the canyons where they lived. This was the power, in the form of mothers and women, that they went deep into the caverns to approach.

They must have clearly perceived the power of fecund nature emanating from the rock walls. They pressed their tools, coated with pigment, toward the invisible, virtual space from which the power came. Only the face of the cavern walls changed as the shapes of animals appeared from the tips of their implements on the surface of the stone. That wall became a boundary surface at which the power of virtual space transformed into a thing of this world, visible and material. At this boundary surface, the power of fecund nature took the form of herds of countless elk and bison.

We might call these activities "magic." It is a mature form of thought that attempts to grasp the change in power that occurs at the boundary between the latent and manifest worlds. During the long period in which humans lived as hunters, this way of thinking achieved a high degree of sophistication. Its purity was seriously compromised by the Neolithic Revolution and the rise of agriculture, but its importance did not fade in the least. It lived on in art. It lived on in the "savage mind" (*la pensée sauvage*), as Claude Lévi-Strauss put it. Today it is once again finding new forms of expression in our contemporary world of technology.

There is a common principle, transcending differences in both time and circumstances, that underlies both the pictures of elk that the people of Lascaux painted on the cavern walls and the "invaders" that appear on a video game's black screen. This can be called, à la surrealism, "magic"; it can also be understood, à la psychoanalysis, as an expression of the *objet petit a*.

That which the people of the Paleolithic era felt as the power of fecund nature, modern urban dwellers have come to feel as the Thanatos drive, which operates upon the unconscious. At the boundary with the unconscious, where the people of Lascaux used their pigments and implements to realize an artistic connection, we now place a television monitor and perform magical rituals adhering to fundamentally the same principles when we stare at the blinking lights that appear and then disappear there.

In this way, the hidden, true form of the *Ultraman* monsters and the invaders becomes clear. These monsters that exhaust the capacities of man's imagination are close relatives to the staggering numbers and varieties of animal shapes drawn on the cave walls of Lascaux, connected by the same principles of magical thinking. They appear from a place that is not of this world, passing through the edges and gaps in our consciousnesses. Moreover, they are unlimited in number and their forms of expression are diverse and manifold.

By drawing on the walls, the people of Lascaux came in contact with the spirit of death and then performed a ritual intended to induce a rebirth that would produce new life. What of the children of our world today? They too, through monsters and video games, come into contact with the Thanatos drive that rises up at the edges of consciousness. Is this paired with the same principle of "rebirth"? Is magic still robust enough to wield such power today?

CHAPTER 3.

EROS, THANATOS, AND RPGS

W hen I was a child, I was crazy about B-grade horror films from the United States and their monsters. Those films all shared one very interesting characteristic: the frightening monsters appeared so abruptly that everyone in the audience was left wondering where in the world they had come from, even though the film itself seemed to ignore this question to focus exclusively on how horrible the monster looked. (Perhaps that was what made them B-grade?)

The movie might go something like this: A happy family comes to the spacious lawn of some park carrying a picnic basket packed with food. Spreading out a blanket, they sit down and begin their pleasant lunch. Suddenly—really suddenly—an unknown creature appears out of nowhere. Completely savage, it attacks the family and begins eating them one by one. The girl screams; her brave father rushes at the creature, only to be immediately devoured. Fear reaches its peak and then the movie abruptly ends.

The first time I saw a film like this, I was dumbfounded by its idiocy. When I look back at them now, though, I feel differently. I now see the monster's sudden appearance as a straightforward and unaffected visual representation of the fundamental nature of the *objet petit a*. The place from which the monster appears does not exist anywhere in this world.

Let me explain more precisely. Our minds are already structured by a system of language that naturally has "edges" and "gaps." We cannot say concretely, however, where these edges and gaps are. We who are within life cannot simply touch the drive to destroy life. We live with a sense that such a thing exists, but it cannot appear in a place that we could specify as "here" or "there."

In fact, the *objet petit a* must appear suddenly, from no identifiable source. *Space Invaders* and the monsters from B-grade films were faithful to that truth. The space from which the invaders appear and to which they vanish does not exist on this side, in our world: by creating this illusion, the game succeeded in opening a new space. It is similarly unclear whence the monsters of *Ultraman* appear. As with B-grade American horror films, the monsters appear in this world abruptly, as though they had been transported here from some completely different space.

This cannot be made into a "story." If the monster were to emerge from a cave or forest, a story could begin with the exploration of those spaces, those special places that are thought of as the depths or the interior of this world. But if the monster appears suddenly, transported into a world of surface alone, with neither depth nor interior, no inside distinct from an outside—as the invaders and the monsters from B-grade films do—then there is no way for humans to invoke the creativity that would generate a story. The monsters can only be fought. Yesterday and today, this week and next, the same battles continue over and over again. Repetition is not entirely without interest, but it cannot lead to a story.

To invoke a story, all one needs do is fold over this naked world of surface only, with no distinct inside and outside, to produce creases, hollows, and gaps. Folding a surface creates an interior. The result is caverns, depths, and a distinction between the region that is exposed and the region that is hidden away in the darkness. This in turn produces the illusion that the path leading into the depths of those caverns forms a labyrinth, beyond which are hidden the mysteries of this world.

The basic structure is completely unchanged. At the boundary surface where the drives of life come into contact with the system of language (symbols), excess life energy appears abruptly in language, consciousness, and the world as an unnamable and unknowable *objet petit a*. If one folds over the world in which that process occurs, various caverns and forests are created, and events filled with mystery begin to unfold in those depths.

At that instant, fantasy begins. This is how stories about protagonists' journeys to discover the hidden mysteries of the world start.

The bare, simple structure of *Space Invaders* then transforms into a role-playing game (RPG). Within these games, the complex interactions between Eros and Thanatos commence.

The protagonists of RPGs undertake many journeys. There are two reasons for this. First, one of the premises of these games is that space in the game's world has not been homogenized. In that world, beyond the entrance to every cavern, forest, basement, or ruin lurks an unknown, gloomy space in the form of a labyrinth, where one cannot see what lies ahead. Upon entering such a "dungeon," one discovers a world controlled by magic and fantasy that does not conform to the commonsense of the outside world. The player, who is the protagonist, and his party of alter-egos encounter "antagonists" and are aided by "helpers" throughout their long dungeon journey. The logic of Thanatos, the death drive, is clearly and profoundly visible here.

Another important reason the protagonists of RPGs undertake journeys is that the story always begins with some sort of "lack." Happiness that once existed either has begun to collapse or has already done so. The protagonist sets out on his travels, either of his own volition or in response to a mission given him by some character or organization, to restore things to a state of completeness filled with that happiness we are told was lost.

For example, in *Kowloon's Gate*, which was created for the original PlayStation, the journey commences with the following preface:

> The Kowloon Walled City, which should be in the realm of Yin, is said to have appeared in the realm of Yang.
> The Supreme Feng Shui Masters, who preside over the wisdom of Hong Kong, are dismayed.
> In the realm of Yin, Feng Shui energy is nowhere to be found…

Should the two realms accidentally meet, what calamity might result?

The only certainty is that it would it would unleash great evil.

The decision of the greatest Feng Shui Masters is this:

Someone must restore Feng Shui to the realm of Yin.

That person must go to the Kowloon Walled City in the realm of Yin and locate the four divine beasts.

This is a mission filled with unparalleled difficulties and dangers.

Failure, however, is not an option.

With that, one young but talented Feng Shui practitioner disappeared from the realm of Yang.

(From the manual for *Kowloon's Gate*, Sony Music Entertainment, 1997)

Before the story begins, happiness, order, and completeness have already been lost from the world. Time is already lost. The search that the player-protagonist is about to embark on is a search for this lost time. RPGs put to use the structure of myths and folktales that mankind has been passing down for ages, perhaps the last twenty or thirty thousand years.

Both myths and folktales have long drawn the energy that propel their narratives forward from this sense of lack. Jack was poor because his father was dead. In an attempt to improve his circumstances, he set out on a journey to climb the beanstalk that grew from his magical beans, arrived at the giant's castle in the sky, and then won a great fortune by defeating the giant. Stories with similar structures can be found all over the globe. Here is one such myth from the Cheyenne people of North America:

Long ago, before the Cheyenne chased down buffalo on horse-back, at a time when they used dogs to pull a sled called a travois, a young shaman was traveling north with his wife, whom he had kidnapped. He was doing so because the land had dried up and stopped bearing fruit, plant life had disappeared, and there were no animals to hunt. After a long journey, they suddenly arrived at a vast forest. In the middle of that forest, a giant mountain rose into the sky, reaching the very heavens. At the foot of that mountain, the two of them found a rock. Rolling it to one side, they discovered the entrance to a cave, which they then entered. Deep in that cave they encountered the great magical spirit Maheo. Together they addressed him, saying . . .

> (Folktale collected in the late nineteenth century by the anthropologist George Dorsey, as cited by Hans Peter Duerr in *Sedna, oder, Die Liebe zum Leben*, 1984 via Kenji Hara's 1992 translation.)

Whether or not the states of lack and need that are the starting points of these stories are based on some sort of reality is not important for the tales themselves. What matters is the simple fact that some lack already exists. Happiness, satisfaction, plenty, order, and the completeness of the world are already lost when the story begins; this point is essential.

The tale begins at the moment the protagonist realizes that the flow and distribution of the energies that created the world are out of balance, and the happiness that once existed no longer does. To put it differently, at the moment that the desire for a tale appears in the hearts of people, the world has already fallen out of balance: when one wants a tale, it is already too late; the original state of completeness has disappeared and cannot be experienced as such again. In acquiring one thing, another is lost forever, without any chance of being restored. This also makes it clear that tales are born of this sort of mental structure. The essence of tales is deeply linked to the formation of the child's mind. All human children contain imbalances within them. They are creatures who became human children by losing something, and so they seek stories.

So, what is it that children acquire, and what do they lose permanently as a result? What they lose is their oneness with their mothers; what they gain, in the language of psychoanalysis, is the state of "castration." Until then, the mother and the child are connected without the mediation of the system of language (that is, prelingually), linked through the rhythms (music) of the mother's body: physical contact with it, its warmth, its motion, its milk. From the child's perspective its own existence is undifferentiable from its mother's; the two are in a state of balance that has its own unique and flexible order. That is, for the child during this period of oneness with the mother, the four classical elements are in balance and neither the energy that pulls inward (Yin) nor the energy that spreads out into the world (Yang) are in excess; instead, the two maintain a cooperative relationship.

However, because humans are creatures that speak, this situation cannot last forever. The mother and child who were in an undifferentiated state must be pulled apart, and the child must enter the world of language. The system of language comes from society. For the child, its relationship with this system is not the sort of caring one it had with its mother; the system comes to the child possessing a frightening power. The child cannot relax its vigilance as it did in its state of oneness with its mother. It must clearly separate from the object. Its mental space will henceforth be structured by this system of language. Moreover, the system of language is bestowed upon it by this unknown entity, "society." It is in this way that the child is "castrated" through a process of internal conflict.

From that point on, the space of the individual's mind ("I") will be structured by the social system of language. At that moment, the state of oneness with the mother suddenly vanishes. In the new mental space constructed by language, memories of the prelingual maternal space in which the four classical elements and Yin/Yang were in balance lose their sense of reality, as though they were from the distant past. In their place, the new social space structured by the system of language (symbols) appears before the child with overwhelming force.

The child, however, senses that there is disharmony somewhere in this new space. This is because the world structured by language lacks the harmony that the child once perceived in the world using the prelingual senses of its entire body. Where things had once felt linked by a single bond, now they are separated one from the other, and the world has lost even the principle that might have bound them together. Here there is no true "I." Harmony, love, and truth are lacking from this world. It is at this point that fantasy is born. The psychoanalyst Jacques Lacan expressed this using the following formula:

$$\mathcal{S} \diamond a$$

This formula should be read as follows: the moment language begins to structure the space of the mind (which occurs when the child experiences castration), the truth of the "I" becomes something without a place of its own. The "I," having been erased in this way from the system of language, desires the *objet petit a* as a way of reclaiming the harmony and integration it has lost. This is because the *objet petit a*, as a remainder that cannot be symbolized by language, reveals a path to this lost world. In this way, the "I" that has been erased from the system of language embraces fantasy in an attempt to recover the lost world where the four classical elements are in harmony.

This power to spin together fantasies, represented by the $\diamond$, is the power that propels stories; it is the principle of Eros. The "I" feels as though it has lost something important, but even the "I" does not know what that thing is. In order to find it, the "I" sets out on a journey, depending upon this *objet petit a* to open a path to what lies outside it in the edges and gaps of the world structured by language.

This is how the stories of fantasy begin. In order for the protagonist to reach the edges of the world, he leaves his town or village and travels to distant lands. When he discovers caverns and tunnels and forests, he casts off his fears and enters them. He does so because these are the gaps, scattered throughout this world, that can provide access to what lies beyond. The goal of the "I" in making this journey is to reach the true "I." Surely that will be a brilliant moment, when a brand-new order is brought once again to this world, restoring the lost harmony of the elements . . .

The power of Eros gives the child, who has experienced castration, the courage to set off on this journey of fantasy, in search of a way to restore "lost time." The child, energized by the power of Eros, sets off on this impossible journey despite living in a world structured by language and being burdened by this disharmony and lack. Absorbed in fantasy, the child must be trying to resist the reality of castration. Eros, using the power of fantasy, attempts to save the child from the state of despondency that would otherwise result.

In order to do so, however, Eros must enlist the cooperation of Thanatos. In order for the "I" to recover the true "I," it must approach the edges and gaps of the world, but what emerges from these places is none other than the life-destroying death drive. By approaching and then passing through Thanatos, the "I" becomes able to approach this "lost time." Eros skillfully uses Thanatos in an attempt to achieve its objective of allowing a person to live within fantasy by adroitly denying the reality of castration.

Here we see all the fundamental components of the RPG. They are the techniques with which Eros uses Thanatos. This becomes even clearer when one applies the "morphology of narrative" as developed in the study of folktales. The protagonist, who has set out on her journey in search of the lost balance and harmony of this world, encounters two types of power in the course of the journey: "helpers," who provide assistance with difficulties and challenges along the way, and "antagonists," who appear from time to time and attack the protagonist in order to stymie her journey. Without defeating (with the assistance of the helpers) the hordes of antagonists that appear one after another, the protagonist cannot achieve her journey's goal: the recovery of lost time.

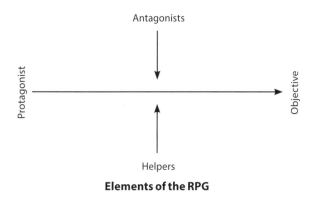

Elements of the RPG

These antagonists bear a striking resemblance to the "invaders" and the *Ultraman* monsters in that they appear suddenly from an unknown source, form ranks blocking the protagonist's progress, and then launch devastating attacks. Over the course of this journey marked by instability, the player-protagonist confronts the death drive, which has the capacity to destroy her. Just as Freud discovered when he observed the *"Fort/Da"* game, children will return again and again to situations that cause them distress. It is possible to see this as an urge the "I" feels to destroy itself.

Children try to direct aggression toward themselves. Why? Perhaps it is because some sort of energy hidden within life longs to destroy the "I" that has been constructed by the system of language. Writhing intensely in the minds of children is an urge to shatter this recently constructed "I" and to return to their original state of unity, in which there was neither separation nor differentiation.

This is undoubtedly the Thanatos drive. However, as Freud put it, Thanatos is an extremely impatient urge. Eros possesses the same desire. Eros realizes when it is already too late that the "I" suffers a definitive lack. Nonetheless, Eros attempts to set out on a dogged journey to reclaim lost time. $\mathcal{S} \diamond a$. Despite the lack, driven by the impossible fantasy that it can recover the lost unity of harmony and space, Eros is determined to continue the long journey of life.

Eros has the same objective as Thanatos. While Thanatos attempts to induce self-destruction in its impatient desire to achieve that objective, Eros aims to realize it in the distant future, at the end of a long, roundabout route. The protagonist who sets out on an adventure in an RPG and the antagonists that attack the protagonist along the way are originally the same; the only difference is the way they appear. The one that chooses a detour on its path to achieving its goals is called Eros, while the one that impatiently races toward its goal directly is known as Thanatos.

In the face of Thanatos's urge to destroy, Eros's protagonist probably would not be able to complete their difficult journey without the assistance of helpers. In folktales, this role is played by fairies met in the forest, generous goblins, or kind monsters such as Falkor, who soars through the sky with the hero of *The Neverending Story* on his back. While this tradition is preserved in RPGs, these helpers are often represented as "powers" or "combat techniques" (as befits a folktale in the age of technology) that the protagonist (or the protagonist's party) acquires gradually.

Powers like this once belonged exclusively to creatures like fairies and monsters, who gained them because they lived close to the edges and gaps of the world. That is to say, these powers are none other than the distinctive magical power of the *objet petit a*. As a result, they are of the same nature as the powers of the protagonist's antagonists. Antagonists use their powers to threaten the existence of the "I," but Eros uses them to protect the journeying protagonist and to destroy the opposing forces.

Thinking of it this way, it becomes easy to see RPGs and the folktales upon which they are based advancing toward a single goal, in a very complicated way, all the while skillfully allocating the desires that well up within life, smashing them into each other, and disguising themselves. That single goal is to pursue a now-lost happiness and then realize a state of absolute contentment that cannot be realized in this world. To this end, Eros mobilizes all the power of fantasy. Even in the present reality, as the balance among the four classical elements begins to break apart and the equilibrium between Yin and Yang crumbles, we are drawn to the fantasy that if we continue our journey of difficult trials without abandoning hope, eventually we will recover a time in which things that are now severed from one another are restored to their original unity.

Thanatos, however, tells us that this is impossible. Fantasy urges the "I" on its quest as though success were possible—but it is not. The lack within the "I" will never be remedied. Eros merely leads people along a detour. Its objective may be the same as Thanatos's, but Eros works to conceal the truth in an attempt to protect the "I" at all costs. Thanatos is impatient and direct, and seeks to destroy the "I" that is filled with the hope that Eros has given it. Each time, however, it is defeated by the protagonist and his party, which includes helpers who are symbols of Thanatos who have gone over to the side of Eros.

According to Freud, both Eros and Thanatos serve the "death drive." RPGs substantiate this claim. In the minds of the children who are absorbed in these games, the impatient urge to destroy the self (Thanatos) and the hope that arrests that urge and attempts to extend life through the protective mechanism of fantasy (Eros) are engaged in a fierce struggle. At the end of the twentieth century, humankind has finally made the "death drive" visible and pulled it to the surface of society. Digital technology made that possible. Ultimately, RPGs aim to embrace the power of Eros and fantasy even as they expose people to the urges of Thanatos. Who can easily deny the truth in that struggle?

CHAPTER 4.

THE TRIUMPHS OF *POKÉMON*

N ow we can finally talk about the great triumphs of *Pokémon*. Before *Pokémon*, the pleasure of video games may have been related to Freud's "death drive," and players may have been enticed by an excess of life energy, unable to be symbolized using the power of language, in the form of the *objet petit a*, but these were not sufficient for the "savage mind" to begin functioning actively in the world of video games. It took *Pokémon* to produce full displays of the savage mind, cultivated internally by mankind over tens of thousands of years but still active and vigorous today.

Of course, these were only the smallest, most simplified fragments of something that had once been more vibrant. As small as those fragments were, however, seeing them in the images moving on that small gaming device was cause for great surprise and joy. Still vital, they drove Japanese schoolchildren mad with excitement. These descendants of mankind's oldest philosophy have not yet been killed off, whether by an environment now dominated by science and technology, a harsh educational system, or mind-numbing media, and their connection to nature is still preserved. This joy is what drove me to write this book.

The game *Pokémon* has succeeded admirably in mastering the *objet petit a*, that troublesome thing contemporary culture has difficulty managing in any area of life. Both in the home and in society, today's culture is rapidly losing its original "castration" function under the oversized influence of developing technology and media. Our system of language has begun to lose its power to structure the space of the unconscious. The authority of the "father" (by which I mean not a biological father specifically but anything with the ability to separate the infant successfully from its state of mother-child unity) has thus far supported the system of language. Now, however, the existence of this "father" is threatened everywhere, both at home and in society at large.

This robs the never-ending series of manifestations of the *objet petit a* that emerge from the gaps and edges of consciousness of their appropriate resting places in the space of the mind, allowing them to float up to the surface and make trouble. To make matters worse, they also grow larger. When the "father" was still present, the system of language (symbols) would initiate powerful mechanisms to repress manifestations of the *objet petit a* to the realm of individual fantasy as soon as they appeared, smoothly managing them so that they did not overflow into the space of society. Today, however, language's "castration" function has weakened, and the things that should have remained in the realm of individual fantasy, overseen by the symbolic order, instead rise to the surface in a world where the boundaries between these realms are no longer clear.

In such a world, the question of how to skillfully manage the *objet petit a* becomes a matter of urgent concern. In most areas, it cannot be done. For that reason, these remainders of the life force flowing unsymbolized from children's unconscious minds inevitably began to be absorbed by the game industry. Various games perform the function of a digital shield for children, absorbing the aggression and eroticism that cannot be controlled. Urges that cannot be controlled in this way flow into the realm of even more pathological junk culture. The education children receive at home and in schools has become incapable of responding to these wild eruptions of the *objet petit a*. This is the fate of a developing civilization; it is inevitable.

And so we must search for a new method of sublimation for these formidable, savage subjects. We can no longer return to the stable family structures of the past and manage them that way. Art addressed this issue early, from the end of the nineteenth century into the twentieth, anticipating the situation that confronts us today and seeking a new way of sublimation-through-expression of these "remainders of symbolization" not captured or suppressed by the system of language or the structure of social authority that develops from that system. Today, in the twenty-first century, it seems hard to claim that the art movements that attempted to confront this change were successful. Contemporary art, in fact, is rapidly losing its capacity for sublimation precisely because of its compatibility with the present technological environment. As the works become elite brand-name goods in their own right, art has actually become even more distanced from the problems we confront.

This is the situation that game designers grapple with. Their job is to provide a single channel for the urges that continue to overflow into children's lives even today but cannot be symbolized and are ignored without any molding, sublimation, or castration. Some designers succeed and some fail, with the latter headed straight for the cesspool of junk culture. *Pokémon* too was born in the face of these dangers, but navigated them with unprecedented success, particularly when it came to handling the unconscious minds of younger primary school students.

The secret to that success lies in the "science of children." For children, science performs the important function of giving them intimate access to the world around them as a rational object, while still maintaining their separation from it. It lets them create a "discrete connection (connected, yet still separate)" with the world. *Pokémon* uses this function of science to convey children safely through the simultaneously fascinating and bewitching realm of the *objet petit a*.

Consider the "scientific" worldview of a child who collects insects. An insect collector has achieved an appropriate distance from bugs and muddy puddles: neither too close nor too far. *Pokémon* is a game created to cultivate that capacity in children, by designers who themselves were once amateur entomologists like this.

Various "savage monsters" inhabit the world of the game. The player ventures through this world, capturing and collecting these creatures, battling them against each other, and overseeing their development. The ultimate goal is to collect one of every kind of

Pokémon in the world and register them in a "pokédex." One guidebook to the game explains it this way:

> "Pokémon" is the generic name for the mysterious creatures
> who live in this world. There are more than 150 different types
> which can be found in diverse places, whether they be land, sea,
> or air. They gain experience and grow when you battle them
> with one another. Even a Pokémon that is weak at first can learn
> powerful skills as it grows, becoming stronger over time. There
> are also types of Pokémon who can evolve and change their
> forms as part of the growing process, or by using certain items.
> (*Poketto monsutā ao: hisshō kōryakuhō* [Pocket Monsters Blue:
> Strategies for Certain Victory], Futaba-sha 1997, p. 4)

The game's designer, Satoshi Tajiri, got the original idea for
Pokémon from the world of television monsters that he had known as
a child. This is how he describes the development of that idea:

> The name of the game I originally thought of was *Capsule Mon-
> sters*. Obviously, I took this idea directly from the Capsule Kai-
> ju, or Capsule Monsters, in *Ultra Seven*. If you could put
> monsters in capsules, it would be easy to collect them and to
> carry them around; even more importantly, you could trade
> them with other people by exchanging data via Game Link ca-
> bles. It would be easy to carry them with you but also to let
> them go. This gradually led to the name becoming *Pokémon*.
> (A continuation of the conversation that appears earlier in this book.)

The Capsule Monsters kept by the protagonist of *Ultra Seven*, Dan
Moroboshi, would emerge and fight to protect him when he got into
trouble and was unable to transform. Because they were not very
strong, they would soon be overwhelmed, so Dan would call them

back and they would return to their capsules. Children really liked the idea of a monster that one keeps as a pet to fight alongside you as an ally. Tajiri and the other *Pokémon* designers belonged to that exact generation of children.

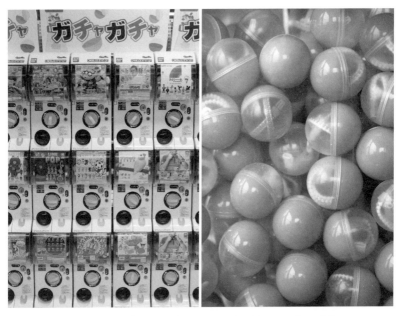

Gacha toy vending machines, Tokyo
Uniphoto Press International Inc.

Gacha capsules with a toy
Uniphoto Press International Inc.

The Capsule Monsters reside in long, thin capsules like medicine ampules. The designers of *Pokémon* probably chose the shape of a ball instead due to the popularity of "gacha" machines at the time. "Gacha" machines, also known as "gashapon" or "gacha-gacha," were a big hit in Japan in the 1970s. They dispensed a clear plastic ball "capsule" containing a miniature toy when you put in a coin and turned the handle. The toys were often quite finely detailed, sparking interest in adults as well as children. They remained popular for some time and have enjoyed a recent resurgence with the development of capsule toys of increasingly elaborate design. It is a real renaissance moment for the "gacha" machine, with everything imaginable being produced in miniature: not just the old favorites like popular characters, food samples, miniature electronics, and dinosaurs, but also goldfish, insects, amphibians, mushrooms, and even monks in conical *fukaami-gasa* hats. These advanced capsule toys, designed so thoughtfully, carefully, and beautifully, are emerging as the rightful successors to the tradition of miniatures that Japan is famous for, such as bonsai and netsuke.

While this comment might first seem to be a casual observation, it speaks to something quite important. Shrinking the monsters to a compact size that allows players to store them in capsules and carry them in their pockets provided them with the very ability that makes today's Pokémon "pocket monsters." The monsters that inhabit the world of *Pokémon* can be caught when a player throws Poké Balls at them. Players are initially given a certain number of these balls by the professor, but later can find or buy more. Once monsters are caught, they can be carried around in these balls and sent to one's computer as data to be stored there. As will be discussed in more detail in Chapter Six, children can also trade monsters from their device to another child's via a Game Link cable.

In another *Pokémon* guidebook, the development of these "Poké Balls" is described as follows:

> While the Pokémon are made up of multiple species, they share many commonalities. One primary example is the ability to be stored in a capsule. Some monsters appear extremely fierce when active, but that fierceness fades and they can be put in this sort of "monster ball" capsule—one of which I have with me here today—when they are sleeping or their strength is extremely low.
>
> I believe it was in 1925 that Professor Westwood, the father of

Pokémon Studies, was performing experiments on extracting Primeape's rage. The professor, who at that time was already around retirement age, mismeasured the medication dose and accidentally weakened the precious Primeape as a result. The Primeape, however, perhaps acting on a survival instinct, slipped into the professor's reading glasses case, which lay next to him, and curled up into a ball. This incident led to Professor Westwood's development of capsules in which to hold Pokémon, along with techniques to capture them. Subsequent improvements to the capsules led to the "Poké Balls" that we have on the market today, which are both simple and effective.

(*Poketto monsutā zukan* [Illustrated Encyclopedia of Pocket Monsters], ASCII 1996, p. 131)

As this passage explains, when the strange creatures known as "Pokémon" exhaust their strength, they roll themselves up into a fetal position in a case or a ball. It would seem that they do not mind being stored in these balls. In fact, they need the capsules as places to rest and recover. From the moment they are born, they possess the capacity to be kept as pets. Even though they can be violent at times, if they are raised properly they can be kept as close companions; if released, however, they will become wild once again. The Poké Balls strengthen the creatures' innate tendency to grow neither too close to, nor too distant from, humans.

How do the natures of the monsters change when they are closed up in these balls? They are "reduced" and "connected, yet still separate." The moment they are put in Poké Balls, these bizarre-looking monsters—which up until that moment had been attacking the players—become docile and begin to obey commands. They also shrink in size and are instantly converted into data.

Monsters who are "reduced" undergo a dramatic transformation, becoming objects that can be manipulated through reason. Anything, when reduced in size and processed as information, can be controlled in this way. Should a giant monster suddenly appear (as perhaps from a field or forest or cavern), we would initially be assaulted by powerful emotions that might prevent us from properly recognizing our assailant. With the passage of a little time, after we examined a drawing or photograph of it, we could then calmly and carefully observe its characteristics. In the same way, this process of reducing and converting the world to data transforms it into an object we can encounter rationally.

In *Pokémon*, such encounters with strange creatures and the subsequent "reduction" that results from capturing them are repeated again and again. Each repetition helps cultivate a reliable response— rational rather than emotional—toward the urges that appear from the edges of the player's unconscious in the form of strangely-shaped manifestations of the *objet petit a*.

Another important thing to realize is that Poké Balls effect a clean separation from the formidable *objet petit a* stored inside. Consider the monster closed up in the Poké Ball: because it is covered in a thin membrane of plastic (the Ball), when one carries it in one's hand there is no direct contact with the sticky and slimy flesh characteristic of a monster. This stickiness and sliminess is the sensation of saliva and of the mother's breast, and thus related to contact between the bodies of mother and infant. The saliva and the breast are at the point of contact between the two; as such, the sensation indicates a particular sense of bonding with the *objet petit a*.

Through the mediation of the Poké Ball, children become able to separate themselves effectively from that bonding, as the dry and smooth sensation of the plastic surface reinforces their sense of separation. Moreover, even though children are separated from the *objet petit a* by that thin membrane, they are still able to carry it around in their hand or bag. As a result, through these Poké Balls they are able to discover the perfect distance, neither too far from nor too close to this troublesome liminal object connected to the memory of contact with the maternal body.

Children must not move too far from these liminal objects. As they are still drawing upon the objects for life energies that have not yet been symbolized or castrated, were they to move too far from them, the children would feel as though they had been rendered completely transparent by the system of language (symbols) and would experience a radical sense of alienation. Nor must they approach the objects too closely, as this would leave their minds forever trapped in the state of oneness with the mother. In such a state, drives that have not been symbolized would be unable to escape the child's world of imagination and fruitlessly reproduce themselves there, rendering the child unable to interact normally with society.

At the age when children become obsessed with *Pokémon*, this separation is a matter of great psychological importance. On the one hand, they still possess memories of the state of physical and mental oneness with the mother; on the other hand, with the pressing demand that they establish a relationship with society, they are also troubled by the need to establish an appropriate distance from the *objet petit a*. *Pokémon* attempts to provide children in this situation with the model for a process that resolves this.

This, you see, is how you capture it in a Poké Ball and establish separation from it, the game instructs them. *But you must not be careless with it; because it is the source of your life force, you must carry it with you at all times. Should you want to store it somewhere, you can transfer it to the* Pokémon *computer. If you achieve this separation and discover an appropriate distance from it, you will become able to render it as data. What do you think? Can you do it? Separate yet still connected, that's what you have to try for, because your life depends on finding that appropriate distance.*

The world of *Pokémon* revolves around creating that appropriate distance between the monsters and the children. That is why the monsters are not just there as opponents to be battled, but also as helpers in recognizing how to feel and think about things. This is a special characteristic of this game worthy of note, especially amid a plethora of other games in which monsters appear suddenly from dark caves, forests, and tunnels and are immediately battled without any concern for their own situation. In order for children to create distance between themselves and these eerie things that are neither friend nor foe, they first battle them. This allows them to distance their conscious minds from the influence of the *objet petit a*. Emotions, however, overwhelm their ability to understand all that is going on and thus comprehend the world of the monsters themselves.

What makes *Pokémon* different is that the goal of battle is not to weaken or kill the opponent, but rather to capture and collect new types. Instead of causing the opponent to disappear, the emphasis is placed on taming them and collecting them in one's Pokédex. This is why the Poké Ball was developed: it makes the wild and difficult-to-manage monsters into rational objects that can be observed.

Prior to that, though, one must not forget that this fictional world was imagined as highly rationalized from the very start, an object of (children's) science from the beginning. The designers' backstory for the game was that Pokémon were originally discovered during the Meiji era (1868-1912) by Professor Westwood, who discovered and documented some eighty different species. His work was continued by Professor Oak, an independent scholar through whose efforts the existence of 151 types (in the first generation) was verified. The point is that the space these Pokémon inhabit was already deeply permeated by the system of scientific language, and the "sticky" connection that is experienced during the period of mother-child unity had been banned from the beginning.

In this world, the magic that fills the *objet petit a* has been rationalized to a certain extent from the start, thanks to those tools of discrete connection (Poké Balls) and the scientifically rational power of Professor Oak. From the perspective of the player, who is the protagonist of the game, Professor Oak is the grandfather of one of their rivals, a boy of similar age who lives in the house next door. That is to say, the player and Professor Oak are not related by blood. They are bound only by a friendship between two people who share the same intellectual passion. Professor Oak never favors his grandson over the protagonist. In fact, he is more solicitous of this intellectual friend than of his own blood relation. Professor Oak, as a representative of the "language of the father," is no less than a stand-in for the power that permeates all realms of this game's world.

"Children's science" —or, in this case, "youth science" —is a type of psychological activity in which one attempts to incorporate the psychologically difficult-to-manage realm of the *objet petit a* smoothly into one's own mental structures by intellectually sublimating it. Doing so weakens the urge to destroy the *objet petit a* and instead builds up a mental bulwark against the eerie pressures of Thanatos that push into the depths of children's consciousnesses. Children set out into nature with the eyes of "children's science." There they are able to experience directly the existence of the maternal "great thing" that envelops them, but they attempt, by bringing the mystery of that "great thing" into the system of language, to discover a mental balance between the happiness they once felt and their desire not to slip back into the paralyzing sensation of unity with the mother. The designers of *Pokémon* were able to rediscover the power of "children's science" that they had experienced in their youth and revive it in a game set in virtual nature. It seems to me that this was an attempt to respond to whatever crises children are confronting today.

"Scientific youth" of the past did not feel much need to worry about this sort of thing. The greatest concern that Astro Boy had was his lack of an *objet petit a*. This android child, born into this world solely through the "words of the father" (scientific technology), had no experience of a state of oneness with the mother. His youth did not include the stage in which the system of language invades the mind, produces a sense of unease, and results in the birth of the magical *objet petit a*. Astro Boy's mind already had a "language of the father" that spoke only of justice. Real humans (including his own real father), however, can never act in strict accordance with reason, because the difficult-to-manage *objet petit a* is always operating in their minds. This seemed impossibly strange to Astro Boy and led him to worry about why the realm of the *objet petit a* had never formed in his mind.

A few decades later, science changed. At the same time, the "science of children" also changed greatly. Many of us no longer believe in the omnipotence of scientific language. We are convinced that scientific language in particular is unable to reach those things that go on in the deepest realms of the human mind. Under such circumstances, the greatest challenge for the children growing up in our world led by science and technology is establishing contact with the magic of the *objet petit a* (which continually arises in all areas of society in a variety of forms) from an appropriate distance. The concerns of "scientific youth" have changed. Those who have been raised in a society of plenty are now worried about an excess of *objet petit a*. Video game designers, too, are trying to respond to that change.

CHAPTER 5.

TOTEMISM TODAY

P eople have long recognized similarities between monsters and angels. Angels have uncommon powers, which give them a monstrous aspect. Monsters, whether brutal or friendly, are pure in their actions, and this evident purity of spirit brings to mind the spirits of angels. The real basis of this impression of similarity, however, exists at a deeper level.

Some theologists teach us that angels were not created by God, but rather that they were beings who acted with absolute freedom in the world that preceded God's creation of the universe. Even after God created the universe (through language), angels found a place in that creation and continued to act freely.

Fluid spirits of freedom—this is the essence of angels. Their appearance is characterized by plurality and diversity. From the "void" that preceded God's creation through language (which cannot be found within that linguistic creation), they appear endlessly, one after another, passing through this world like elementary particles. Because they have bodies of brilliant light, one might imagine that they are all more or less the same, but that is not the case; close attention to the details shows that no two are the same.

Monsters share the same characteristics. We have explained monsters using the ideas and vocabulary of psychoanalysis. The idea of a monster is part of the large genre called the *objet petit a*, which itself is directly connected to the unsymbolizable urges that remain unincorporated into the system of language. These urges begin to operate in the prelingual mind and body before language systematizes the mind. The *objet petit a*, as something that was active in the child's body well before the universe of the spirit was "created" by language and continues to operate afterwards, emerges from the edges and gaps of consciousness in a variety of forms.

Like angels, these forms are characterized by multiplicity and diversity. They are bizarre, unique, grotesque, and filled with originality, inspiring both fear and laughter simultaneously. Left to their own devices, they emerge endlessly from the edges of consciousness. The unsymbolized life energy they bring with them forms a region of "wildness" there that teems with vitality even within consciousness.

The commonalities between monsters and angels are even clearer in the case of "Pocket Monsters." *Pokémon* tries to rationalize, or subject to "children's science," the world in which monsters live. Angels are symbols of the rational portions of the fluid energies that overflowed in space before creation. They represent the lively intellectual activity, filled with curiosity, that becomes difficult for the adult mind to perceive.

The contributions of Professor Oak and the capacity of the Poké Balls effect an appropriate amount of rationalization in the *Pokémon* universe. This prevents children's minds from being accidentally dragged into the depths of the psyche, producing fetishisms. This resembles the way angels, made of rationalizable power from the prelingual world, soar lightly through our own, unlike the demons who are forced into the gloomy darkness. When power from before the creation of the world causes attachments to material, demons are born. This is a result of dualistic thinking. Conversely, when that power causes deliverance from the material world, angels result. In this sense, both demons and angels come from the same source.

Perhaps, then, Pokémon are something like the angels of the world of monsters. The spirit of "children's science" makes possible the sublimation of the *objet petit a*. This allows the creation of a world of magnificent geography along with an ecosystem with an equally magnificent classificatory system that resembles that of true science.

For children, monsters are both frightening and fascinating. Children are exceptionally attuned to the mysterious space of power that lies behind monsters, exceeding both understanding and control. The *objet petit a* that represents the remainder of symbolization leads children to feel that vast expanse of power (intensity), which of course is neither visible nor concrete and can be neither clearly perceived nor comprehended. Because that power cannot be controlled, it is free; because it does not take any clear form, it is fluid; and it is both fascinating and frightening, just like an angel.

Structuring that space is the first task of the game designers. They must draw a map of the space within which the game unfolds. Drawn on a map, it seems to be an oscillating body, constantly vibrating ever so slightly. This space of invisible and symbolic power is still virtual. Change is underway throughout it. The *objet petit a* seeks to emerge from that virtual space through the edges and gaps of consciousness, taking a variety of monstrous forms as it tries to spring forth in endless series into the realm of the actual. At those moments the "Pokémon" monsters appear before children in an attempt to show them that this space in the depths of their minds is not a realm of chaos but a rich and diverse place with an order of its own, despite its complexity as a free, fluid thing.

This diversity is expressed through the variety of Pokémon "species." As in the natural world, individual Pokémon are given species-particular traits and together make up an ecosystem. Professor Oak has already begun creating a detailed classification system of the "Pokémon world." His system divides the 151 species of Pokémon (in Generation I) based loosely on the primary settings in which they live, such as on land, in the water, in the air, on mountains, in grassy fields, or in caves. There are also some monsters living side-by-side who are of the same species but at different stages of evolution.

In this game designed by those former bug-catching youths, the concept of species is given definitive importance. More than anything, the various species of monsters attempt to express in a charming and skillful way a diversity that could be called the game's latent space and which is bursting with free and fluid prelingual urges.

The types of monsters that populate this world were not born independently (with exceptions such as Mewtwo, which was created through genetic engineering), but rather came into existence to express the substance of a single whole through a complex and diverse process of differentiation. Moreover, by limiting the number of species to 151, the game design makes it clear that this diversity is only superficial. All of the species appeared in the world as an expression/differentiation of a single totality of free and fluid power.

Clear principles of division underlie this expression and differentiation. When those divisions are made using the diversity of the natural world as a model, the diverse world of "Pokémon" emerges. One could say that the "Pokémon world" is the result of the abundant dynamism of virtual space revealing itself using the natural world as a model. Playing the game, children learn about the ecology and characteristics of the monsters through the work of battling and capturing them, experiencing one type of "nature" as they do.

It may seem unimportant that Pokémon expresses the diversity of the *objet petit a* with the diversity of the natural world as its model, but this is actually an important fact. It is related to the question, "What is 'nature' to the living creatures we call 'humans'?"

The *objet petit a* is no less than the unsymbolized remainder of life energy showing its face in places like the edges and gaps of consciousness. Children (boys in particular) first discover those gaps and edges in their own bodies and are both drawn to and excited by them. They become objects of intense interest. When children grow older and their spheres of activity expand, they are driven by the urge to discover such gaps and edges in the world around them. This is when children become aware of the existence of the natural world around them.

Boys at this age often become absorbed in collecting insects or crayfish. It is also around this time that they begin to undertake "adventures" with their friends, visiting spaces like old air raid caves in nearby mountains or abandoned sewer construction sites. Children are thrilled when they discover such gigantic gaps and edges in nature. Their mothers may have told them not to go into dangerous places like these, but they are unconsciously tempted to approach and delve into these places in which the secrets of their hearts are hidden, even if it means violating their mothers' prohibitions.

Perhaps those secret places contain something hidden from them by the system of language given to them by their parents and society—something that might even be their true selves. When we who have become adults circle around edges and enter into gaps, we know from the start that it is nothing but a fantasy. For children going into a cave, however, or embarking on a long journey with a friend and coming across a dead body in a forest (in *Pokémon*, as the protagonist is heading off on his adventure, his mother is watching the film *Stand by Me*, which, needless to say, revolves around children who set out to see a dead body), the urge to roam the edges of the world is strong, and does not yet know failure.

This is nature for children like this. For young human beings whose conscious is still unsullied, nature is an interface between the world created by language and the separate realm (or spirit world) that is outside that system but nonetheless perceptible. Because nature, with its insects and crayfish and strange plants, functions as a place of gentle connection between language (things that have been symbolized) and that which language has not integrated into itself, it has attracted children since the beginning of time. Nature is one giant edge, a gap of unfathomable depth, that children find irresistible.

Here we see the phenomenon of a layered interface. The nature created through anachronistically simple pixelated images on the tiny screen of a hand-held game device functions, because of its extreme artificiality, as an interface between real nature and the nature that exists in the minds of children. Inside the game device, the unsymbolized life energies that make up nature in children's minds are happy to find appropriate expression by taking the form of monsters. Then those monsters themselves perform another interfacing function, expressing desire created by the imagination, using the real natural world outside as a model.

In the minds of children, when the natural world outside appears in the form of a monster, it re-creates their own actual experience of nature. Poliwag, with its transparent stomach, and its evolved form, Poliwhirl, were designed to evoke the strangeness of the tadpoles ("polliwogs") children encounter in real life at the water's edge in spring. Reptilian monsters like Charmander, Charmeleon, and Charizard also seem familiar to them thanks to the "World of Giant Reptiles" exhibits sometimes held in museums and the imaginary biology presented in Spielberg's *Jurassic Park* and other dinosaur films. The pixel art icons for these creatures vividly connect children's experiences to real nature through the medium of the imagination.

Poliwag (left) and Poliwhirl (right)
©1995 Nintendo / Creatures Inc. / GAME FREAK inc.

This creates a circle, linking the "nature" of children's unconscious, the "nature" of the real world, and the "nature" created by the game.

When children become enthralled in collecting insects or catching crayfish, an internal interface is always created between the nature within them and real nature, no matter how small or unnoticed. External nature is not a simple object to children, as it is when it is subjected to scientific scrutiny or development for profit. Instead, it is the *objet petit a*. The feel of dirt and water, the sliminess of mud, the sensation of crawling around in tall grass, the scary tingle of taking a bug in hand, the twitch of the rod when a fish takes your bait—all of these have a connection to the prelingual mental and physical sensations experienced during the period of mother-child unity.

When a child seizes a frog, his unconscious thrills at the contact with the *objet petit a*. When a child walks through the mud, the feel of it squeezing between her toes recalls to her unconscious the memory of a time when she was not yet separated from the world. Nature ceases to be an object; the edges of the system of language and the gaps in the world transform themselves.

The game, the child's unconscious, and real nature form an intimate bond in this peripheral realm. Real nature provides the model for the Pokémon universe the monsters create, and because that process occurs in this peripheral realm it also becomes a powerful model for the expression of the child's unconscious. The diversity of real nature is the model for the diversity of the monsters, which in turn is the model for when the "free and fluid power" presents itself as diversity. Real nature and the unconscious create a circle through the medium of the computer.

The world of *Pokémon* is a world of classification. Because it is small and has already been observed, recorded, and classified by Professor Oak's scientific reasoning, there already exist illustrated guides describing the 151 species of Pokémon in great detail. Every monster was born of the free and fluid power that lies behind that world. That power possesses an original continuity, but each time it produces a monster, a rift opens, making it discontinuous. In order to express these discontinuities symbolically, the Pokémon world displays a maniacal passion for classification.

The concept of "species" plays an important role here. For example, the species of Pokémon that follow all share the same "water's edge" biome.

Oddish	Bellsprout
Gloom	Weepinbell
Vileplume	Victreebel

The six "grass type" Pokémon who are poisonous and live in "water's edge" biome

These classifications are not arbitrary. They are an attempt to introduce discontinuities through the creation of a diversity of species into the field of the free and fluid power perceived directly as emanating from a biome like the water's edge. Lévi-Strauss wrote the following about this sort of passion for classification:

> The importance of the notion of species is to be explained . . . by its presumptive objectivity: the diversity of species furnishes man with the most intuitive picture at his disposal and constitutes the most direct manifestation he can perceive of the ultimate discontinuity of reality. It is the sensible expression of an objective coding.
>
> (Lévi-Strauss, *The Savage Mind*, p. 137.)

The creators of the game, by providing their small fictional world with a full 151 species, are trying to introduce a rift of discontinuity into the fluid stream of life. This gives children, who can perceive the continuous latent power flowing behind that rift, a taste of the rational pleasure of turning chaos into order. The diversity of species expresses the diversity that pervades the living world in direct imagery, and this arouses the pleasure of the "savage mind" in children, who love things like illustrated guides. Children's science is enamored of classification, and Pokémon makes full use of this fact.

Looking more closely still, each species of Pokémon has its own particular attributes and engages in what anthropologists call "joking relationships" (relationships in which individuals can tease one another) with others. No monster in the *Pokémon* world is ever indifferent to any other. Encounters inevitably become engagements, whether in combat or mockery. And even as they scowl at each other in the fearful moments of a battle, they will continue the joking relationship. Engagements always lead to a calculable outcome, and to ensure this, each species possesses its own particular attributes.

More concretely, each Pokémon is assigned one or two of the following types:

O=Normal	I=Ice	S=Psychic
F=Fire	B=Fighting	M=Bug
W=Water	P=Poison	R=Rock
T=Electric	G=Ground	Y=Ghost
K=Grass	H=Flying	D=Dragon

To give a few examples, "water type" Pokémon live near the water and are good at swimming. Pokémon modeled on birds are "flying types." "Grass type" Pokémon who live near the water have the ability to "absorb."

For this reason, when monsters of different species encounter one another and enter into a joking relationship, the outcome can be known with certainty. Were a "fire type" Pokémon such as Growlithe, who can wield flames in combat, to enter into the joking relationship known as a "battle" with Squirtle, the latter could use an attack known as "water gun" to deliver significant damage. However, were Squirtle to turn the same attack on a "grass type" opponent, it would cause no damage at all, because grass is compatible with water. The relative strengths of all fifteen types are shown in the table on the next page.

As you can see, the seemingly bewildering combinations are actually based on the same fundamental principles as rock-paper-scissors or the Five Elements used in Chinese divination. In the case of rock-paper-scissors, the outcome of any two of the "types" (rock, paper, or scissors) entering into a joking relationship is easily determined. With the Five Elements, the number of types increases, but any given combination still has an established outcome. *Pokémon* has more types yet—fifteen, in all—but the outcomes can be determined using the game's many-valued logic.

Compatibility Combinations of Types

		Attacked Pokémon Type													
		O	F	W	T	K	I	B	P	G	H	S	M	R	Y	D
Attacking Pokémon Type	O	•	•	•	•	•	•	•	•	•	•	•	•	×	▲	•
	F	•	×	×	•	◎	◎	•	•	•	•	•	◎	×	•	×
	W	•	◎	×	×	×	•	•	•	◎	•	•	•	◎	•	×
	T	•	•	◎	×	×	•	•	•	▲	◎	•	•	•	•	×
	K	•	×	◎	•	×	•	•	×	◎	×	•	×	◎	•	×
	I	•	×	×	•	◎	×	•	•	◎	◎	•	•	◎	•	◎
	B	◎	•	•	•	•	•	◎	•	×	•	×	×	◎	▲	•
	P	•	•	•	•	◎	•	•	×	×	•	•	◎	×	×	•
	G	•	◎	•	◎	×	•	•	•	◎	•	▲	•	×	◎	•
	H	•	•	•	×	◎	•	◎	•	•	•	•	◎	×	•	•
	S	•	•	•	•	•	•	◎	◎	•	•	•	×	•	•	•
	M	•	×	•	•	◎	•	×	•	•	×	◎	•	•	×	•
	R	•	◎	•	•	•	◎	×	•	×	◎	•	◎	•	•	•
	Y	▲	•	•	•	•	•	•	•	•	•	◎	•	•	•	•
	D	•	•	•	•	•	•	•	•	•	•	•	•	•	•	◎

◎ ... Very effective   × ... Not very effective
• ... Effective   ▲ ... Not effective

**Relative Strengths in
Rock-Paper-Scissors**

**Relative Strengths of the Five
Elements used in Chinese
Divination**

What is Pokémon trying to convey to children by expanding this system? Monsters battle with outcomes determined by this chart of relationships. These battles may seem to encourage aggressive impulses, but these seemingly unrestrained attacks are actually a type of joking relationship based on a clearly determined logic, each and every operation of which allows children to observe directly the dynamic movements in the world of "diverse power" that operates behind those logical relationships. Battles become acts of perception, and attacks simultaneously function as expressions of love for the opponent.

The world of *Pokémon* is a virtual one, created within the computer by logical operations. Its deft connection to the unconscious minds of children, however, lets it successfully extend its influence to the vital forces that still elude the process of symbolization there. It molds children's unconscious minds like clay, producing rifts that create discontinuity and scenes of encounter between qualitatively different powers.

The surprising result of this is that, through computers, the "savage mind" begins to operate within the children's minds. This oldest form of human philosophy, which allowed people to interact fully with the richness of nature with no connection to technology whatsoever, suddenly comes alive again in the minds of the children who hold this game in their hands. Their latent power of the "savage mind" has not died, despite the changes to nature itself and the attempts of education to wound their minds. How ironic that a computer game should reveal this to us! The ideas put into this game by its designers, who grew up while the suburbs were expanding at a startling rate, seem to be accurately grasped by today's children too, who are forced to live within a much more menacing environment where the relationship between nature and man has become bizarrely complex.

We have come to see in some detail how the video game *Pokémon* employs this method from the science of children to adroitly avoid the fetishization of the *objet petit a*, which is so seductive to children, and allow children to perceive the free and fluid power behind each individual Pokémon. In the language of sociology (or at least the newly founded sociology of the nineteenth century, as expressed by Auguste Comte), we might describe this process in the following way:

> When, for example, the similar vegetation of the different trees in a forest of oaks had finally to lead to the representation, in theological conceptions, of what their phenomena presented in common, this abstract being was no longer the fetish belonging to any tree; it became the god of the forest. So the intellectual passage from fetishism to polytheism is essentially reducible to the inevitable preponderance of specific over general ideas.
>
> (From Auguste Comte's *The Course in Positive Philosophy*; quote taken from *The Savage Mind*, p. 164.)

In the "forests of *Pokémon*," each monster grows in accordance with a common model for calculation. As the language of psychoanalysis would put it, each of the manifold representations of the *objet petit a* exists and grows in the world of the game with the support of a common power. That power comes from the life beyond the edges of consciousness, and reveals not individual creatures or monsters but abstract life itself. This is the "god of the forest" in the world of *Pokémon*, supporting a polytheistic mentality.

Just as what is referred to as the "savage mind" attempts to understand the "god of the forest" that exists behind the diversity of species and goes by such names as "Hau" and "Mana," I cannot but perceive the existence of something similarly vivid behind the world of *Pokémon*. This sense is not mine alone; many children share it.

A number of the children with whom I spoke about the game told me about how, after becoming enthralled by it, they had begun to be plagued by the feeling that strange creatures like Pokémon might suddenly jump out of small groves in their neighborhoods or grassy areas in parks. For these children, the "polytheistic sensibility" in the game had begun to operate in the real world! Anthropology is the study of the present above all, and the "savage mind" continues to grow densely in places like this. This fact alone could be the starting point for entirely new ethnographies of totemism today.

CHAPTER 6.

THE GIFT AND THE WORLD OF GAMING

M ore than anything else, it is trading that most characterizes *Pokémon*. The handheld Game Boy devices on which the game is played can be connected using a link cable, allowing a player to either send a Pokémon from her device to another or receive a Pokémon that she wants. In this way, the game expands from her closed individual world into her connections with others.

Few contemporary inventions could be of greater interest to anthropologists than this. An anthropologist who learns of this sort of exchange would no doubt feel as though she were among Native Americans early in the twentieth century hearing about the famous "potlach" ceremony. This custom was created to help people escape isolation and venture into a larger social network by ritually gifting their prized belongings to others and receiving gifts in return. The close resemblance to Pokémon trading reminds us that we are still in the midst of the "savage mind."

What were the game's designers thinking when they struck upon this idea? Consider this detailed account from Satoshi Tajiri:

Today we have networked games that operate via the connections of the computers on which they are played and so on. I see this as the natural evolution of earlier interconnected games. In these games, simple data, such as the player's coordinates and speed, were exchanged to allow players on multiple devices to compete. *Pokémon*, however, went beyond this. The data exchanged using the link cable is invisible, but the player feels as though living Pokémon are traveling between the devices. This is similar in feel to bartering. Home video game consoles produce a deeply immersive and solitary experience, but games that use link cables have the power to produce a different experience. This is because they are able to function as tools of communication.

(Quoted in *Poketto monsutā zukan* [Illustrated Encyclopedia of Pocket Monsters], ASCII 1996, p. 125)

Tajiri explains that he and the other designers struck on this idea when they were looking for a way to transform the deeply immersive and solitary experience of home video game consoles into a method of communication. This is the moment that the strange sensation of sending living Pokémon via link cable to another player's device was born. Tajiri describes this sensation as reminiscent of bartering, which is a valuable insight. Put more precisely, it approximates the sensation that accompanies the act of gifting.

The act of gifting involves a special feeling that does not accompany the exchange of commodities or the simple bartering of objects. Commodities are not invested with the individuality of the person selling them. In fact, only objects that have been cleansed of the individuality of their previous owners—who lack any such attachments—can become commodities. In the case of gifting, though, an aspect of the giver's essence inevitably remains attached to the gift. Gifts are, in fact, precisely those objects that have been infused with someone's essence in this way.

When Pokémon are traded, a similar transfer of the original owner's essence takes place. The Pokémon that a player catches in fields, forests, and caves become "infused" with that player's name and ID. No matter where a Pokémon is traded through the circle of exchange in the game, it will always bear part of the essence of the "parent" who caught and raised it.

There are even times when a Pokémon "adopted" from another player will not listen to its new owner. Here, too, the essence of the original "parent" remains. In the case of a commodity, once it has changed hands it ceases to be the property of its previous owner and belongs to its new owner free and clear. The exchange of both gifts and Pokémon, by contrast, is designed to *avoid* this simplicity.

Connected Game Boy devices
GAME BOY is a trademark of Nintendo

In the "savage mind," things are not merely things. The possession of a thing involves the absorption of that thing into one's essence. Before taking a possession to the market to sell as a commodity, the possessor must perform a ritual act to divest the object of his essence. On the other hand, if he wishes to gift the object to a person he considers important, then the essence of the giver infused in the object is gifted along with the object itself. Put differently, the act of gifting involves imparting a portion of the giver's essence to the recipient of the gift.

When one uses the link cable to exchange monsters in *Pokémon*, the logic of commodified society is repudiated and the "savage mind" revived. The designers who created the game understood this through the term "drama."

The strength of *Pokémon* is its ability to produce drama outside of the game. When a person gives a Pokémon bearing his name

to someone he is fond of, or when a person lends a strong
Pokémon to a friend in exchange for a bowl of ramen, these are
examples of the possibilities hidden within the game for drama
that goes beyond its bounds.

(*Poketto monsutā zukan* [Illustrated Encyclopedia of Pocket Monsters],
ASCII 1996, p. 125)

"Producing drama" refers to something happening, something
moving. Data moves through the link cable. This data is nothing
more than ones and zeroes. For the people playing the game, though,
what is moving through the cable is a thing of great importance. It
could be a gift, which one player deems both desirable and precious
and the other player is gifting to him out of kindness. The people
playing the game understand that this is the sort of exchange that
is taking place. At such moments, people who are actively partici-
pating in the game feel that something else is passing through the
cable alongside the thing being exchanged. One might refer to this as
"essence"; one might also refer to it as "spirit."

This "essence," or individuality, is a very mysterious thing. Though
it is nearly impossible to say precisely what it is, we all have many
moments in our lives in which we feel that our "essence" has come
into contact with the "essence" of another to whom we are linked by
friendship or love. In those moments, something moves across the
gulf that separates us as discrete objects.

This movement could be called "drama"—a movement that causes
the heart to race and occurs in our world. When we feel whatever it is
that moves across the gulf between us as discrete objects, no matter
how faintly, we experience a strange happiness that transcends calcu-
lations of profit and loss. This experience has yet to be sufficiently
explained by either philosophy or psychology. Only anthropology
has engaged in ongoing research, dating back many years, into this
phenomenon. Anthropology, which is profoundly interested in the

"savage mind," has come to recognize that the sensation of happiness and plenty that people feel at such moments is somehow related to the phenomenon of the gift.

With the buying and selling of commodities—the simple movement of things—the phenomenon of the gift does not occur. For an exchange to become an act of gifting, the individuals involved must be able to perceive the attendant movement of a virtual power that resides in the items being exchanged. Individuals guided by the "savage mind" referred to this as the "spirit of the gift."

Feelings of plenty, happiness, and "drama" can be felt in the human world when one initiates the movement of this invisible, latent power, known by such names as "Mana," "Hau," and "spirit." This includes times when the god of the forest directs the flow of this power toward the human world in the form of prey to hunt; it also includes times when power flows between communities or individuals and leads to the creation of ceremonies to break down the manifold barriers built to separate them.

When one encounters this universal power, whose flow transcends individuality, profound meaning can arise with the exchange of words and things. When this sort of connection is lacking, however, only a simple and shallow exchange occurs, in which things and people are reduced to numbers and information. A deep exchange of meaning—true "communication"—does not occur.

When the game's designers decided to try to make *Pokémon* a "communication tool" through the adoption of the link cable, they naturally but perhaps unintentionally stepped into this realm of "the gift" as studied by anthropologists for many years. "Deeply immersive and solitary" forms of play like those offered by home video game consoles—or by auto-eroticism for that matter—usher one deep inside a single space where this sort of flow does not occur. In this situation, only the communication between the player and the game continues, intensifying the closing off of the individual. While this might result in a rich imagination, it rarely produces the joys of sociality.

In the world prior to the mass commodification of video games, however, children naturally followed their unconscious drives and participated in makeshift "gifting" of their own. The game's designers say that they made the game "with the thoughts they themselves had as children at the forefront of their minds."

Sugimori (character designer): For example, we thought that a game where one could show off and exchange the rare things one discovered would be fun, didn't we?

Tajiri: *Dragon Quest* had a rare item called a "magical hat," and you said that you had two of them. I played the game for days trying to get one, but I just couldn't. I remember thinking, *If he has two, I wish he could give me one.* More than wanting to make an RPG, in the beginning I really just wanted to be able to trade things. The RPG elements and raising monsters—all that came later.

(*Poketto monsutā zukan* [Illustrated Encyclopedia of Pocket Monsters], ASCII 1996, p. 140)

The entire world of *Pokémon* originated in the idea of exchanging the *objet petit a*. This was also a nostalgic experience for those who had been children before video games. In the poverty-stricken Japan of the immediate postwar, *menko* cards had given them this experience. When another child had a *menko* card you wanted, or if you had multiple cards of the same value, you would trade with someone else. Over time, *menko* were replaced by *Kamen Rider* trading cards and other fads. Trading important manifestations of the *objet petit a* lets children develop bonds of friendship.

Perhaps children hoped to initiate some kind of flow between themselves and other children by gifting them with an *objet petit a* that was also a fragment of their own life energies. Exchanging *men-ko* cards or Poké Balls containing Pokémon allowed unsymbolized remainders not captured by the system of language to flow between them. At these moments, a qualitatively different, deeper kind of communication occurred than the kind adults mean when they tell children to "play nicely." The connection itself is short-lived, but the memory of something important having passed between them lasts forever.

If we were to call the flow of desire not incorporated into the system of language "spirit" and the *objet petit a* "the gift," nearly everything I have said so far about *Pokémon* parallels the main themes of gifting as researched by anthropologists. Just as desire runs throughout the mind and body, the free "spirit" that rules over the act of gifting is ubiquitous, running through all things and bringing life energies to the world. It is the remainder that cannot be incorporated completely into the world of humans through symbols. For that reason, this freely flowing "spirit" could also be called a universal drive.

It is not easy to give away an *objet petit a*. They are filled with the memories of our most important desires, and when we give them to another person, we give a part of our essence too. The same emotion emerges from any act of giving. To a greater or lesser extent, each and every time we engage in gifting we experience the feelings of people with "savage minds" when they "gave" their daughters, whom they had raised with such love and care, to other men in marriage. It follows, then, that a "gift" occupies the position of the *objet petit a* for society.

Pokémon was able to achieve an unanticipated profundity by reviving in video game form the strange and rich experience that children once enjoyed in their forms of play. Today, with all areas of society on the verge of being absorbed into the logic of commodities (creating a world in which people, too, having been definitively alienated from one another, are exchanged as commodities), the game has the ability to restore another, qualitatively different logic of exchange to the hearts of children—one from the distant past.

A world in which relationships between people are not formed solely according to the logic of commodities has been given new life among children. It would be a mistake to dismiss this as nothing more than a game. Human children are born into this world with the seeds of the "savage mind" already sown in them. In a society like ours, whose wealth "presents itself as an 'immense accumulation of commodities'" (Karl Marx, *Capital*), these seeds are exposed to great danger, whether because they have been sown in barren soil or because they are at risk of being cut down by education, media, or the family the moment they sprout their first leaves.

In such a moment, the world of games functions as an asylum for the "savage mind." Just as with every other asylum, it is filled with serious risk of decay or defeat. Still, from time to time a great work appears. Hope always exists, even amid the gravest peril.

Epilogue

The epigraph of this volume is a memorable sentence from Claude Lévi-Strauss's 1962 *The Savage Mind*. In that book, Lévi-Strauss provides many interesting examples of the "savage mind" continuing to thrive in the contemporary world.

The desire to make detailed miniatures of real buildings and cars; the naming systems used for pet dogs and race horses; the unconscious rules that influence the thinking of a chef as she prepares and serves food; the folk logics underlying customs such as children receiving presents for Christmas; the stereotypical thinking that politicians are prone to fall into; and the joy of watching films with a happy ending . . . Along with these other activities, Lévi-Strauss also directs his attention to the origin of the mental structures that make card games and ball games so enjoyable.

The Savage Mind was written half a century ago, but its message has not aged at all. To the contrary, it grows more relevant by the day. It touches on those things that are most important if humankind is to have any hope of surviving the twenty-first century.

Trying to imagine a situation in which the savage mind has been completely lost from humanity results in only bleak images. The savage mind, including the capacity for myth and art, represents a storehouse of potential. It allows mankind to create things and to perceive directly this lively process of creation that makes the world more than a giant information object or collection of copies.

Of course, during the contemporary period in which homogenized education and a media industry attempting to completely commodify people's sensibilities and thoughts are spreading at a speed and to a scale that is nearly unimaginable, the savage mind is increasingly losing its proper place within society. Even so, as the commodification of people's unconscious minds continues (a process that began a century ago with the invention of film, accelerated by the commercialization of Christmas in the United States, and now enters its final phase with current computer technology), a staggering number of new video games are released on a monthly basis, sucking money out of the wallets of both children and young adults.

Without a doubt, video games are enjoying a golden age. At the same time, though, it is hard to say that these games will provide the human psyche with fertile soil for the savage mind to germinate. Many of those precious seeds have been cast onto poisoned soil and produce only the fruit of aberrant desires.

For this reason, the case of *Pokémon* is a truly rare one in this world of ours. I have no hesitation calling it the best example of what Lévi-Strauss described as the savage mind that is thriving in the contemporary world. Although the game was created by adults who once had been insect-collecting children, the ones who discovered the game's appeal were the children themselves. How has *Pokémon* seized the hearts of children to the degree it has? In search of the answer to that question, we found ourselves wandering even into the deep forest of the unconscious.

And it really is a deep forest of the unconscious. We discovered two important ways of thinking there. The first was the idea contained in the notion of "the god of the forest" from the nineteenth-century sociologist, Auguste Comte. According to his theory, children who become obsessed with collecting insects and plants do so because, whether they realize it or not, they perceive the vague presence of "the god of the forest" in them. Such children enjoy observing nature and are aware that there are many "species" in the world of plants and insects. Those who feel a deeper oneness with nature detect behind this profusion of species an abstract "god of the forest" that gives birth to and nurtures all these different plants and insects.

The attraction of categorizing lies in the way it allows us to embrace the functioning of precise knowledge as we perceive this presence (what Heidegger would refer to as *physis*, or being-itself) behind the diversity of species, without falling gradually into mysticism. *Pokémon* is designed to let us feel the presence of this sort of "god of the forest." Its classifications do not merely occur in accordance with some cold operation of the intellect. In *Pokémon*, the passion for classification metamorphizes the *objet petit a* into diverse monsters. Behind these monsters, never emerging to show itself, is the abstract "god of the forest."

Another important idea for *Pokémon* is "the spirit of the gift," to borrow a term from anthropology. The "exchange" that occurs through the link cable produces a strange sense of satisfaction for the children involved as something good moves between them. One child unhesitatingly relinquishes something dear to himself when his friend needs it; the other, upon receipt of such a freely given treasure, realizes that he should reciprocate with something equally precious: this is the generous cycle of "gifting" that occurs through the cable.

When Japanese children of the late twentieth century participate in an exchange with this sort of mindset, a "spirit of the gift" is in operation that closely resembles that of Melanesian or Native American peoples of the past, like a sort of positive energy flowing between people. In these moments, children can feel those positive things move in their hearts and gain a feeling of satisfaction, much as those "primitive peoples" did.

We can sense these ideas of a "god of the forest" and of "gifting" at work in *Pokémon*. Adults made the game. Yet the children who received the game quickly understood that an excellent opportunity had arrived for the "savage mind" that had been waiting inside them for an opportunity to sprout, and soon began developing ways to make use of it. It is true that the game is a commodity, but the children who received it rapidly set about customizing it. Unlike adults, who tend to use devices as their manufacturers specify they should, children became absorbed in individual and unique methods of *bricolage*.

Players may give the Pokémon they catch whatever name they please. One type of Pokémon, of the Hypnosis type, has the species name Drowzee. A player who collects her own Drowzee can give it an individual name such as "Sleepyhead." Pokémon who have been named are drawn out of the classification system and given an individualized link with the player, who is the protagonist of the RPG. Merely by giving their Pokémon names, children customize the classification system.

When children form teams made up of their best Pokémon, they engage their creativity. Because each Pokémon is of a given species, each of their special powers (called "moves") has strengths, weaknesses, and particularities. To build a team balanced enough to cover a variety of possible combinations, children must draw on a surprising amount of knowledge. Thus, children dedicate a great deal of thought into customizing their teams' powers.

In battles, strategy is essential. One goes into battle after skillful strategizing, using one's full knowledge of the classification system to determine which species will prevail over the opponent's Pokémon. Here too, one cannot just follow some predetermined strategy. There is no single answer that constitutes the best approach; in fact, strategy can only be thought of as something one must customize. What is of most interest is that in *Pokémon* strategy must be formulated using the logic of the game's complicated system of classification. The system of classification that is written into the body of the "god of the forest" only appears in the real world once it has been customized.

Moreover, the "exchanges" conducted using the link cable function to customize relationships between children. In the world of children, the "gift relationship" exerts a powerful influence on friendship bonds. Because they are aware that the "spirit of the gift" cannot easily or quickly be set in motion, they give their precious Pokémon only to carefully chosen individuals.

This is quite a strange situation. Few adults have any idea that the savage mind is flourishing so richly among children usually no older than the fourth grade. Children are thought to be strange if they have not completely cleared their minds of such "primitive" thinking through a packed and rationalized educational system and discipline at home that is severed from the traditions passed down from ancient times. Rather than vanishing from this society, however, such thinking is thriving with increasing vitality thanks to one game.

Seeing this situation brings to mind the striking final scene of the film *Pom Poko*. The *tanuki*, or Japanese raccoon dogs, who have been engaged in a desperate struggle with the humans and their ongoing development of the nature around them, realize that their resistance is futile and decide to enter human society in order to survive. They transform into salarymen, riding trains on their commutes into the city. On moonlit nights, however, they gather secretly in a nearby park, let their tails down, and make merry with their *tanuki* dance . . .

Children are like these *tanuki*. They seem completely assimilated to the world, attending school during the day and cram schools in the evening, but when parents and teachers are not looking they peer into their little game devices, through which the savage minds that lie dormant within them dance and secretly revel in the mysteries of moonlit nights. Our society, in which everything has been commodified and made subject to science and technology, denounces such activity as unnecessary or perhaps even harmful. Children, however, do not let this bother them, and continue attempting to speak to mankind's oldest philosophical abilities, which still lurk quietly within them.

Long ago, people tried to forbid children from approaching things that were simultaneously alluring and dangerous. Adults would tell them, "Don't just go whistling at night; if you do, something will drag you into the darkness!" Their logic was as follows: children have the same characteristics as the period just after sunset does; therefore, if they were to whistle at dusk or address the darkness, they might be sucked into that dangerous interstitial time.

Aristotle writes something similar. Analyzing the injunction to adults that they not allow children to drink alcohol, he realized the following: children possess the same characteristics as alcohol, so recklessly allowing them to drink will strengthen the element of fire within them to a dangerous degree. Children are fire; therefore one must not allow children to drink "firewater."

When we see adults today trying to keep their children from becoming obsessed with games like *Pokémon*, this seems to resemble these examples but is actually the exact opposite. It is not that parents realize that children possess the essence of the "savage mind" within them and hope to prevent reckless contact with it. Rather, they disapprove because they believe that children should be training for the exceedingly rationalized thought of adults, and think that momentarily fixating on an illusion like this is not good for the healthy development of the intellect and will not be an experience useful for them in society later in life.

The "savage mind," though, while it may appear capricious and lacking in seriousness, is one important form of intelligence about the links between humans and nature. It does not objectify nature in the way science does. As a result, the nature outside us creates a "place of free and fluid energy," with neither an inside or outside, by opening another "nature" within us. To observe is to be observed; to speak is to be spoken to. The "savage mind" is the type of intelligence that operates precisely in spaces like this.

This type of intelligence produced a game in which children who have lost their place to be active discover another place where they can trust in their own capacities—a place where they can express themselves. I was quite moved by the fact that the adults who dreamed up a place where this can be expressed so well, in a form of intelligence that has such a long pedigree, were none other than the Japanese.

I can say with confidence that this is a form of genius specific to the Japanese. Had it not been within our culture, which has seen a singularly high degree of achievement with regard to the molding and treatment of the *objet petit a*, it is unlikely that a rebirth of the savage mind with this degree of refinement could have occurred. Important things are always casually drifting around in places like this, and it is children who tend to be the ones to discover them. These discoveries then grow along with the children themselves. It is my hope that they will not be applied toward the charmless ambitions of adults. It is also my hope that this "savage" spirit will overcome the formidable obstacles it faces today and remain with us well into the future.

Afterword to the First Edition (1997)

This is the second time I have written something somewhat serious about video games. The first followed the release of *Xevious*, more than a decade ago. As a former fan of *Space Invaders*, I was surprised to see these simple but mysterious games suddenly evolve so dramatically; that led me to attempt an analysis of shooter games through the lens of myth. It was during that project that I discovered how interesting it was to talk with game designers. The stories I heard from the designer of *Xevious* (translator's note: these are included as an appendix in the current volume), Masanobu Endō, gave me the idea of games as things that mold the unconscious.

After that, I turned away from video games for some time. I was unable to muster much interest in the RPGs that were becoming so popular, and did not delve into them deeply aside from noting the release of some new game from time to time. During that period, however, video games made remarkable progress. With the introduction of the use of polygons, computer graphics technology matured significantly, and a number of excellent games were released during that time. While I was by no means a good gamer myself, it became impossible to remain uninterested in the developments that field was seeing.

It was when I became aware of *Pokémon*, in 1997, that my love for games was rekindled. The first to bring it to my attention were editors of children's magazines. They got quite worked up telling me that if I did not know this game I could not possibly understand the culture of elementary school students, and that if I didn't understand that culture I could not understand the future of Japanese culture itself.

Still somewhat skeptical, I decided to begin playing the game. Before long, the obsession with games that I had begun to forget was once again roused in me. I became an insect-collecting child in virtual space and poured more than one-hundred hours of play into the game, spanning the Red, Blue, and Green (available only in Japan) versions. I dedicated myself to it until I had collected 125 species of Pokémon (which elementary-school-aged "masters" of the game apparently consider a "so-so" level of achievement.)

I wrote this book based on that experience and with the help and cooperation of many people. First, I must thank my "teacher" in *Pokémon*, Hirofumi Miyazaki (a fourth-grader at the time.) When I got stuck in *Pokémon Red*, the first version I played, he helped me by generously sharing a number of the game's "secrets," leading me into the depths of its world. He also taught me what one might call the "elementary school students' philosophy of *Pokémon*." The ideas in this book's chapter on classification and logic in the game owe a great deal to thoughts he developed through hours of solitary reflection.

Although it was not until I began writing this book that I first met *Pokémon*'s designer, Satoshi Tajiri, when we finally did meet I felt I knew him already. He is a deep thinker who can express things precisely and elegantly. I am amazed at what he and his fellow designers achieved (and continue to achieve) and believe it to be one of the most creative and thoughtful accomplishments of Japanese culture today. Yoshinori Yamamoto of the editorial staff at *Famitsū* (ASCII), Takeshi Miura of the editorial staff at *CoroCoro Comic* (Shogakukan), and Akio Ueno and Takashi Hirayama of Shogakukan all were of great help to me. It is thanks to their help that I was finally able to realize my long-held dream of writing about my own "savage mind" in this unexpected form. To all of them, I would like to express my deep gratitude.

APPENDICES

Appendix 1. *Pokémon GO*, or, The Dream of the Good Walker

July 2016. Shinjuku Gyoen National Garden was enveloped in a strange air that night. Despite the late hour, crowds of people gathered around the periphery of the tree-filled grounds of the park. It seemed as though a vast number of torches were burning in the darkness, looking just like the floating lanterns set adrift on dark rivers to send off the spirits of the dead during the Obon festival. Drawing closer, I realized that the pale lights all came from smartphone screens. The amassed crowds were all staring intently at their phones.

All of these people were beginning to play *Pokémon GO*, which had been released that very day. The young couple next to me had been staring at their screens in silence for some time. Looking at the man's phone, I saw the familiar face of the character Raticate from the *Pokémon* game. The man, facing the Raticate, threw a Poké Ball at it awkwardly, still unfamiliar with the technique, and failed to capture it. The Raticate then vanished into the nearby grass. The other people standing there in the dark were all going through the same motions, wordless and intent on catching Pokémon. Amid the bustle of Shinjuku, the environs of the park were shrouded in a strange silence that must have been baffling to passersby, especially those with no knowledge of the game.

The assembled group suddenly began moving. Phones in hand, they headed for the park gates, which at that hour were already closed.

When I heard people begin whispering "lots of Pikachu are over by the gate!" to each other, I realized what was going on. In *Pokémon GO*, the types of Pokémon that spawn and the location of their spawning change depending on the time. Players move quietly from spot to spot in real space in chasing these locations.

Having already downloaded the game myself, I began to play. My location as determined by GPS was displayed on the screen along with nearby PokéStops and Pokémon spawning locations. The player approaches Pokémon by moving through real space. Using the game's augmented reality mode, the game's on-screen background changes to the actual scene as captured by the phone's camera. This produces the strange sensation that living, wild Pokémon have actually appeared in the real world. Though fully aware that it is an illusion, one nonetheless feels a compulsion to reach out and touch them. The first Pokémon I caught in a Poké Ball was a Doduo.

Battles between monsters and players do not occur in *Pokémon GO* in the same way that they do in other *Pokémon* games. Instead, the role of the Poké Balls (slightly physically larger in this game than they were in the past), has increased dramatically. Battles only occur in Gyms, which have been placed at various locations. By winning a battle and taking over a Gym, one gains the XP (experience points) that are necessary to level up. Players befriend monsters by tossing them treats like Razz Berries, available at the various PokéStops, and then capture them in Poké Balls. Each time a monster is captured, a player's experience points (and eventually his level) increase. In the *Pokémon* game for the Game Boy, players gained more experience when they battled against opponents' monsters who used elemental attacks, such as "water" or "fire," but in the gentler *Pokémon GO*, levelling up is solely a function of how many monsters one captures.

Ingress

Poké Balls were already important items in earlier iterations of *Pokémon*. *Pokémon GO* does away with the RPG component from those earlier iterations and replaces it with the real-world movement of players, tracked using GPS. In *Pokémon GO*, which limits the battles based on a classification system revolving around natural elements to the battles that take place in gyms, the theme of walking around with the monsters you have collected in plastic vessels takes center stage.

The most prominent characteristic of *Pokémon GO* is the fact that one plays it by walking through the real world. This is because the game was built upon augmented reality technology adopted from another game, called *Ingress*, which was created by the American company Niantic.

A few years ago, when *Ingress* was just becoming popular, I tried it out. I soon realized that a game with such depth would be impossible for a lukewarm gamer like myself.

Ingress game screen display

The complexity of the gameplay goes without saying, but I also found it physically tiring. The way *Ingress* works is this: one attempts to control special spots called "portals," determined in real space by the game, in order to create a control field for one's faction by linking three portals into a triangle. It is not enough just to stroll around: one can only take control of a portal by actually walking to the site and attacking it. By the time I had succeeded in reaching my first portal, radiant with XM energy, and turning it my faction's color through various challenging means, I was soaked in sweat, the sun was setting, and I was starting to get lost. The whole experience left me dazed. Moreover, not all the players around one are allies. At any moment agents from another faction might attack and recapture the portal one has just gone to so much trouble to take. As a result, not only is the body fatigued, the mind does not get a moment's rest either.

Exhausted, I quickly retreated from the battle lines, leaving the battle for the future of humanity to my younger friends, and repaired to a nearby café. Having recovered somewhat with a cup of tea, I began spinning various wild ideas—as is my wont—about this fascinating game.

Ingress is an example of a territory game.

Before the game begins, the player must choose between two factions, green or blue. Both factions are battling for hegemony by stealing a mysterious substance (XM, or Exotic Matter) that has the ability to impact dramatically the evolution of the human race, but they differ in what they believe should be done with the substance. The radical green faction, also known as "The Enlightened," believes XM should be quickly utilized to evolve humanity. The moderate blue faction, "The Resistance," thinks that the use of XM should be limited because of the danger inherent in sudden change. Having chosen their factions, players begin a heroic struggle in a world divided into allies and enemies.

Through the use of AR, the battlefield for this struggle is irresistible because it is overlaid on to the real world as represented through Google Maps. In the worst-case scenario, one could easily find one's own neighborhood surrounded by the enemy. When I saw that a nearby shrine I visit regularly was completely occupied by the green faction, I was left with mixed feelings. Would this shrine, a real place filled with a spiritual energy, have its power added to the accumulating energies that were to enlighten the human race? This was a rather unpleasant idea to me, feeling like the exploitation of local power as an energy resource by some global corporation.

What if the whole world were to be divided up into two colors, green and blue, in this way? Imagining this made my head spin. The designers of the game had really set something off in my mind.

Benandanti and *Malandanti*

Gamers are not known for enjoying the outdoors, and *Ingress*'s success at dragging them outside was quite an innovation. Dedicated players would apparently roam the streets every night and occasionally even gather together to hold meetings of a sort. The game itself strongly encourages cooperative play among multiple players.

Nocturnal meetings, roaming groups, individuals engaged in a battle invisible to people who live in the daytime world—while thinking about these images, the word *benandanti* came to mind. The gamers of *Ingress* closely resemble the *benandanti*, groups of people in medieval Italy who possessed special knowledge about plants, animals, minerals, and weather that the average peasant did not and were thought able to ensure a successful harvest through spells and pagan rituals. The word comes from the Northern Italian *bene-andanti*, or "good walker," and they were so named because they would walk through the night, led by their witch leaders.

There were also "bad" walkers known as *malandanti*. They were witches too, but unlike the *benandanti*, who strove to protect the harvest, the *male-andanti* were thought to do bad things such as wither crops and turn wine sour. It is not clear who these individuals might have been, or if they even existed, but whenever something bad beset the village, people attributed it to the *malandanti*.

The *benandanti* often held meetings on Thursday nights. They would lie down on beds, leave their bodies in spirit form, and then set off for meetings in distant fields, riding on the backs of animals like rabbits and cats. There they would enter into individual combat with bad witches from the *malandanti*. Our good *benandanti*, facing the encampment of furious *malandanti* brandishing corn stalks at the other side of the field, would stare them down with fragrant stalks of fennel in hand. If the *benandanti* win, then crops will be bountiful; if they lose, the village will go hungry. What they are engaged in resembles play, but it is play upon which the survival of the village rests.

The *malandanti* likely do not exist. The *benandanti* who have gathered in the fields, however, "see" through the power of their visions these men and women with sinister intentions gathered to attack them. Whichever side overcomes more opponents through battle with fennel and corn and occupies more territory is the victor.

This is where the *benandanti*'s "night battles" share a significant commonality with the players' territory-occupying battles in *Ingress*. The schema of magical skirmishes like those of the *benandanti* may have been integrated unconsciously into the minds of *Ingress*'s designers. Just as those witches from the Middle Ages waged battle with fennel stalks, these *benandanti* of today war against an unseen enemy armed with softly glowing smartphones. The objectives of modern gamers and medieval witches are different, but they are similar in that they utilize an augmented reality that blends reality and fantasy to act as is appropriate for their times.

The mysterious presence that drives the world of *Ingress*, XM, is a homogeneous and abstract form of energy. This previously unknown substance is not given a material form, making it all the more uncanny. Perhaps the reason I find something lacking in the game, as excellent as it is, is due to this monotheistic monotony. By contrast, Pokémon take diverse forms that even now continue to increase in variety. Pokémon are also a mysterious kind of energy, but they are based on the principle of fecundity, of endless divergence and proliferation, where XM converges into a single, transcendent point.

XM is dangerous: when exposed, it has dramatic effects on those around it. Pokémon, on the other hand, are protected, in multiple senses, when they are gently encapsulated in the shelters known as Poké Balls. More importantly, however, the cute forms of the Pokémon themselves play a protective role. Their rounded shapes recall infants and stir up the desire to protect them. In reality, these adorable appearances are a form of camouflage meant to deflect attention from the horrifying "power" that lies within them.

Pokémon stored within Poké Balls are similar to the *benandanti*, who were said to be born wrapped in a caul. People were chosen to become *benandanti* at the moment of their birth. Babies who were born wrapped in their amniotic sac were said to have been born "wearing a hat and shirt," and to be destined to become *benandanti* in the future. Because their connection with the world preceding their birth was unbroken, these babies were thought to possess mysterious powers. As they were thought to remain wrapped in an invisible membrane even as adults, they were connected to supernatural power that ordinary people could not touch. Poké Balls, too, prevent the Pokémon and their unknown energy from inadvertently coming in contact with the outside world. When players find themselves in danger, Pokémon emerge from these capsules to fight on their behalf; after concluding the battle as quickly as they can, they return to their capsules to rest.

The Contemporary Nature of Territory-Occupying Games

Games based on occupying territory have a long history, beginning with Go, which was created in ancient China. Video games of this type appeared in the 1980s and became a popular genre.

What sets off the mad "territory battles" between allies and opponents in *Ingress* is the mysterious substance XM. The substance possesses the prodigious power to accelerate the evolution of humankind. Those who gather the most of this substance that was previously unknown to humankind will have the power to rule the world. The differences between the two competing factions, radical and moderate, are not great. There is no distinction between good and evil, and even players know that the green and blue factions are ultimately separated only by color. The green faction might be called "the Enlightened" and the blue "the Resistance," but in reality there is no reason to choose one over the other. What is important is the division into two warring factions to do battle.

In traditional festivals, this "dividing into two factions and battling" played a particularly important function. As people's emotions rise, the community splits into opponents and allies and then fierce battles or competitions of strength begin. For example, festivals in Japan climax with the clashing of portable shrines or a race to see which can reach the shrine precincts first. Such competitions are believed to jostle awake the gods that reside hidden in the depths of the shrine's main hall, restoring a healthy vigor that the village community was beginning to lose. Perhaps it was for the same reason that the people of medieval Italy regularly conducted the rituals of battle with the *malandanti*.

The designers of *Ingress* may have sought to recreate this sort of ritual in the present day in order to rescue a world that has found itself at an impasse. Territory-occupying games take on new meaning in today's world, in which the Cold War structure has collapsed. With the end of the Cold War, which saw the world divided into Eastern and Western camps, humanity seemed on the verge of salutary growth. However, when the walls fell and the monolithic logic of global capitalism swept the globe, the world instead was plunged into conflict and discord.

"Dividing the world into two parts and having them battle" is no longer a binary scenario but a space of the unknown, possessing non-integer dimensions. Because battles do not break out when the world is dominated by a uniform "1," nothing new can be born in such a space. Neither would anything happen if the world was a uniform "0." Barrenness alone reigns. It is necessary to divide the world into two and set those sides against each other. The battlefield is neither "1" nor "0"; neither is it "2." As the tug-of-war continues, the front lines separating the two camps' territories are constantly shifting, and the game's battlefield transforms into a dynamic space whose shape and dimensions are always changing.

It is at this moment that a heretofore unperceived power can be felt to begin operating through this dynamic space. Before the division into two warring camps, that power was repressed by a rigid world system and kept below the surface. When schisms appear and battles begin, however, a dynamic space that had not existed before that moment begins to move. It becomes possible to detect eruptions of once-invisible energy and power. At the front lines of territory-occupying games, elements appear from dimensions that did not even exist before, and hitherto unthinkable world reforms become imaginable.

Rendering this fascinating mechanism of "territory-occupation" physics visible is an incredible achievement by *Ingress*. The multiple battle lines of the game are drawn simultaneously on real maps all over the globe. The size of the occupied territory is not the issue. What matters is the regional characteristics and intensity of the control fields that are constantly being formed by multiple agents. On this pretext, the game draws people out into the world and has them participate in something they would normally never do. It may appear that players are engaged in some recreational pastime, but hidden in the game is a more deliberate and positive intention. One's opponents in the game are not actually opponents, nor are they the Other; they might instead be thought of as a different, hidden self. Dividing into enemies and allies and battling is a way of renewing the world; while it might appear to be battle, in fact something more creative and cooperative is taking place.

A Future Created by Good Walkers

Inviting Pokémon into the platform created for *Ingress* created a strange mismatch. A better fit might have been a game based on *Harry Potter*, with its canonical worldview of good and evil. *Pokémon* contains few dichotomous or territory-occupying elements. Even in *Pokémon GO*, in which players divide into teams that battle for control of gyms, their function is limited.

Winning battles and amassing power are not the main goals of *Pokémon*. At the center of the *Pokémon* worldview is an entirely different principle. What the player in *Pokémon* is striving for is to collect as many Pokémon as possible and then carry them around with him in Poké Balls. Unlike the dead specimens in display cases of an obsessive insect collector, however, these are "living" Pokémon whom the player raises and names as he will: he not only collects them but also takes good care of them. He can then carry them around, trade them with friends, and battle them against other Pokémon. Depending on how the player raises them, each individual Pokémon develops different characteristics even from others of the same species. Rather than bragging "Mine is the strongest Pokémon in the world," players take pride in their particularity: "My Pokémon, which I raised, is unlike any other." Rather than being "number one," players strive to make their Pokémon the "only one." This is the principle that is valued above any other in *Pokémon*.

As a lyric from one *Pokémon* song says:
> Magikarp, the weak Pokémon,
> Weakest Pokémon in the world,
> Magikarp, my Pokémon,
> I'll train you as you are.

A Magikarp has almost no strengths of its own, but if you carry it around long enough it will eventually evolve into the fierce Gyarados. For some reason, though, there are many fans who do not like it when their Pokémon become stronger. The game designers have gone so far as to create a "B button" option that will stop the evolution process, just for fans such as these. Rather than Gyarados, whom they do not find cute, they prefer the weak and frail Magikarp: "I like my Pokémon just the way it is." To be honest, I am among their number too.

Games in which enemies are vanquished using force are not very popular in Japan. Rather than wanting to grow stronger, *Pokémon* players enjoy collecting various rarities and trading with their friends, even if they remain weak. They earn respect for having collected an array of rare Pokémon rather than for being strong. Victory is not determined through something as simple as power; even in competitions for superiority over an opponent, ingenuity and a diversity of interests are desired. *Pokémon* battles are not about knocking out one's opponent, but befriending them through the interaction. And what one tries to befriend is not just the other human players but the many living things hiding in nature, such as insects, birds, and fish.

There is one more principle that is fundamental to *Pokémon*: that it is small and easily carried around. Ever since its original appearance as Game Boy software, portability has been an essential element of the game. *Pokémon* got its very name from the idea of "pocket monsters" stored in small capsules convenient for collection and exchange that can be carried in one's pocket. The pleasure of going outside with a friend carrying your Pokémon in your pocket is just like the pleasure of setting out on a picnic with a small basket filled with delicious treats, and children would not trade it for anything.

The joy of carrying around something you love in a light-weight, high-tech vessel: our first experience of this was the Sony Walkman, which was released at the end of the 1970s. "Walkman," as the name suggests, is a tool used while walking. People loved using the small audio player as company when they walked, jogged, or cycled. When we walked the streets while listening to music that flowed through its headphones, the scenes of commotion in the real world overlapped with this music that seemed to come from another dimension, creating the strange sensation of a reduplicated world. This, I believe, was the earliest prototype for our experiences with AR.

Following the Walkman came the iPod and then the iPhone, leading to the spread of smartphone culture through the world. *Pokémon GO* was born when this culture merged with that of *Pokémon*, which had developed on portable game devices from the same inspiration as the Walkman. The process was both extremely natural and inevitable. The ability to play *Pokémon* outside was a precondition for its creation; moreover, the game was designed to allow multiple players to exchange data via the game link cable. Children are extremely perceptive, and there is no way they would miss this function. Elementary school children spontaneously began to gather on school grounds or in parks in order to trade and battle Pokémon with their friends. These activities can be said to have anticipated the socially networked communication that *Line* and other programs have made so central to our daily life today.

From the earliest stages, *Pokémon* was designed to leap out into the streets using this mobile environment. Even when it was a black-and-white eight-bit game, it gave a strange sense of floating in a space between the real and virtual worlds. VR that allowed one to experience virtual space by putting on goggles already existed then, but that replaced the real world entirely: it was impossible to experience a multilayered reality simultaneously. The elementary school students who played *Pokémon* at that time, however, had found a way to experience the multi-stratum expanded reality that we now call AR without ever being taught how.

In *Poketto no naka no yasei* [The Wildness in Your Pocket] (1997), I first wrote of my suspicion that some new ability was emerging in the children I observed moving between reality and the world of the game. These children who were obsessed with Pokémon shifted at will between two different layers of "reality": the virtual space in their portable game devices and the real space that lay before their eyes.

When I began playing the game, I too began to have moments of excitement when it felt as though a Raticate or Diglett might leap out at any moment from nearby grasses or gutters. If an adult could feel this way, imagine how much more the hearts of children, with their greater sensitivity, must have been quivering with anticipation.

Is the boundary between the virtual and the real as stable and certain as people believe? In the minds of the modern person, an ontological inversion between the two is underway. That which occurs in the virtual space of the game is not simply a pleasurable pastime; it can become an effective tool to change the real world. Reality does not influence the game; instead, the game actively alters the real world. This is what the global hit *Pokémon GO* teaches us.

Reference: Ginzburg, Carlo. *The Night Battles: Witchcraft and Agrarian Cults in the Sixteenth and Seventeenth Centuries*. Translated by John and Anne Tedeschi. Baltimore: Johns Hopkins University Press, 1983. Originally published as *I benandanti*: Ricerche sulla stregoneria e sui culti agrari tra Cinquecento e Seicento (Turin: Giulio Einaudi editore, 1966).

Appendix 2. The Game Freaks Who Play with Bugs

In 1967, the large American amusement device manufacturer Williams Electronic Manufacturing Company released a pinball machine called *Shangri-La*. By that time, the pinball industry was already well established. Pinball machines, first produced in the mid-1930s, had evolved at a similar pace to the United States economy to become one of the best-known types of electromechanical game machine, alongside electronic bingo and slot machines.

Shangri-La offered no particularly noteworthy innovations in its mechanical aspects. In fact, it was rather commonplace. A ball shot by a plunger rolled down the slanted playfield; the player used flippers located on either side of the playfield's lower edge to knock the ball back up the slope and score points by hitting targets (which propelled the ball back using electromagnetism). Most pinball machines shared this design, but each manufacturer strove to vary and intensify the player's experience by changing the layout or number of elements or adorning the machine with a variety of lights.

In this sense, *Shangri-La* was a relatively simple machine for its time. The scoreboard was not decorated with complex, flashing lights, and the cabinet did not even have a third flipper. What seems to have drawn people's attention was the truly unusual illustration decorating the scoreboard.

On the right is a water bird playing in a pond surrounded by a profusion of lotus flowers. Standing by the pond are three beautiful "oriental" women with narrow, slanted eyes, wearing Chinese clothes. A Chinese-style temple stands at the pond's source. Considering these elements alone, the image might seem to possess a certain cultural unity. However, the questionable nature of the design emerges when we notice beyond this a torii gate of a Japanese shrine surrounded by tropical vegetation. The sense of incongruity only increases when we look at the left side of the scoreboard. Here we see a kind of multi-storied temple, with men and women on each floor wearing the traditional garb of Tibetan lamas and gazing out into the distance. Following their line of sight we find a large, snow-capped mountain in the center of the scoreboard. Given that the machine itself is called *Shangri-La*, this is presumably meant to be the sacred peak Mount Kailash on the border of Tibet and India.

The name *Shangri-La* comes from the Tibetan word *Shambhala*. Shambhala is an earthly paradise from Tibetan folklore, believed to lie somewhere in the highlands of Tibet to the northwest, in the direction of Mount Kailash. Shambhala became more widely known as "Shangri-La" through James Hilton's 1933 novel *Lost Horizon*, a bestseller later made into a musical and a film. From that time onward, Shangri-La entered the popular imagination as a paradise infused with a seductive orientalism.

The *Shangri-La* pinball machine brims with a unified image of paradise that comes from this strange mishmash of Eastern exoticism in the background. The anthropologist Michael Oppitz writes that the scoreboard is a remarkable representation not only of pinball machines themselves, but also of the essence of capitalism at that time, which underlay pinball's success.

It is immediately obvious that the pleasure of pinball derives from the pleasure of competition, in this case competition with the machine itself. The player controls the ball, which seems to fall randomly, by operating flippers on both sides of the machine. The player's skill level is reflected by means of a numerical score displayed on the scoreboard. Oppitz interprets the pleasure gained by playing as adroitly reflecting dreams of capitalism during a period of high growth. In "Shangri-La, Le Panneau de Marque d'un Flipper" (The Shangri-La inside the Pinball Machine), he writes:

> Pinball attempts to give the principle of competition a new form in a truly skillful way. The catchphrase "the joy of competition is both fun and relaxing," given to pinball games clearly reveals the sense in which it is an unusual variation of a collective game. Pinball creates a sense of society, it is a pot that stews sociality. On first glance, players seem to be striving to reach the highest score by and for themselves. At the same time, though, they play within a social network. Though a pleasant diversion, the machine also possesses a therapeutic function. In the actual workplace, the principle of competition wears down the workers' body. Here though the same principle of competition is tinged with the glow of paradise. Through this therapeutic effect, pinball smoothly slips into the player's mind the goal of "success, success" that society constantly beckons us toward, and then allows that now-relaxed mind to return once again to the competition of real life. In this way pinball can also be seen as a type of

educational device based on the joy of play. On this point in particular, *Shangri-La*, which is shot through with society's principle of competition, stands in sharp contrast with the Shangri-La drawn from the Tibetan legend of Shambhala, which seeks to nullify the principle of competition itself. Both, however, definitely pursue a middle ground. In the paradise of pinball, only the highest score earns a prize. Here too, the maxim "play for play's sake" is alive and well.

Here, as he considers the true nature of the contemporary gaming industry, Oppitz is making an important observation that is profoundly connected to the modern transformation of the concept of paradise as represented by Shangri-La.

The paradise depicted in the Tibetan legend of Shambhala is the source from which all contemporary life—the "here" and "now"—is born; at the same time, however, it can also be thought of as a "Neverland" that one can never actually reach. No matter what form paradise is given, it remains something that can never be realized or observed. At the same time, however, life in this world cannot be understood without this concept of an unrealizable and unobservable paradise. This is the lesson of Shambhala.

On the other hand, insofar as capitalism causes us to harbor the illusion that Shangri-La can be realized in the "here" and "now," it fundamentally changes the concept. We think that "Neverland" is real and will become part of the contemporary world—as a high score displayed on the *Shangri-La* scoreboard, for example. This climbing numerical value that directly quantifies a player's skill is clearly a simple expression of the fantasy of paradise realized "here" and "now," and that realization is deeply interwoven with the principle of competition.

The *Shangri-La* pinball machine expresses, in condensed form, the popular spirit of the heyday of electromechanical gaming machines. In it, competitive capitalism does not yet show even the slightest of ominous signs. This is clear in the strange hodgepodge of Eastern exoticism depicted on the scoreboard. Through the principle of competition, endlessly seeking expansion, the Orient is torn into fragments and then thrown into the American cultural amalgam. The melting pot of this amalgam is the matrix of capitalism's fantasy of Shangri-La.

However, what *Shangri-La* displays in such a clear way are characteristics common to all game machines of the electromechanical period: mechanical movement, a stochastic worldview, and the transformation of players' abilities into high scores. The large-scale changes that were occurring within capitalism were not yet visible in these electromagnetic game machines.

That change was already occurring within the gaming industry, however. In 1962, five years before the release of *Shangri-La*, a student in computer graphics at the Massachusetts Institute of Technology named Stephen Russell had begun developing the first videogame to use a CRT screen as the playfield. That experimental game, *Spacewar!*, had a powerful influence on the gaming industry as a whole.

In January 1962, Russell succeeded in producing a dot that could move across the CRT screen attached to MIT's PDP-1 minicomputer. It took only a month for him to morph this dot into a spaceship, insert stars, add a second spaceship, and then make it so that both of the ships could be controlled to fly around the stars. Not only did the game already have the torpedoes that would be characteristic of later games like *Space Invaders* but also the panic button that allowed players to jump to a random point on the screen. As this suggests, Russell's *Spacewar!* game was already quite advanced.

Nonetheless, it took nearly a decade for videogames to reach a general audience through the gaming industry. This delay had less to do with challenges with computer graphics technology than with financial issues. Because of the expensive materials needed for the transistor logic circuits used by the games, even if they did sell well it was hard to see how they could make a profit.

The challenge was to create a popular computer-and-CRT videogame, with a healthy balance between novelty and familiarity, that could still turn a sufficient profit. It was not until 1972 that this challenge was met by Nolan Bushnell's company Atari and its legendary *Pong*.

The concept of *Pong*, from the perspective of videogame technology, was quite rudimentary, even when compared with *Spacewar!* It was an abstract simulation of table tennis, with two paddles which the players moved up and down the screen using dials and a ball to hit back and forth between them. The game, which a middle-schooler today could program easily on a home computer, probably became so popular precisely because of its simplicity and level of abstraction. Selling nearly 100,000 units (and perhaps double that number if knock-offs are included), Atari and *Pong* were profoundly significant for the gaming industry as a whole.

Changes in arcades, which to that point had been dominated by electromagnetic games like pinball, bingo, and slots, began to appear around 1973, when large-scale game machine companies began producing videogames. A number of companies specializing in videogames also appeared. The mechanical sounds that had filled the arcades were gradually supplanted by humorous and upbeat techno-sounds made by computers. The videogames released by the industry after the success of *Pong* quickly progressed toward increasing complexity and innovation.

The first successful games were all abstract simulations of sports such as ping-pong, tennis, soccer, and hockey; for a number of years after the release of *Pong*, games merely modified the "paddle and ball" game form and introduced increasingly complex movements.

The challenge that lay before videogames was to break out of this format. Companies tried transforming existing arcade games into videogames, but the results, which included racing games and baseball games, did not have a significant impact on the development of the industry despite enjoying modest success. This was because the real charm of videogames does not lie in simple simulations of reality.

Most people agree that Atari's hit 1976 game *Breakout* was the game that truly revolutionized the industry. At first glance it seems to be little more than a clever twist on the "paddle and ball" format, but within its design lay a marvelous idea that became the impetus for true innovation in the industry.

After pressing the start button on *Breakout*, a wall made of bricks appears in the upper portion of the screen. Below, the "paddle and ball" familiar since *Pong* appear and the ball begins to glide slowly down the screen. By moving the paddle left and right, the player bounces the ball up to hit, and in so doing eliminate, each brick. As the game progresses, the paddle shrinks in size while the ball accelerates and moves in increasingly complex ways.

Breakout did not attract much attention upon its release. Few recognized the significance of the ball's ability to break through the wall by eliminating bricks. As the game became more popular, however, people began to realize how important that concept was. What if the program were designed to move the wall up and down, left and right? This idea took the videogame industry by storm, leading as it did to games like *Space Invaders* (1978).

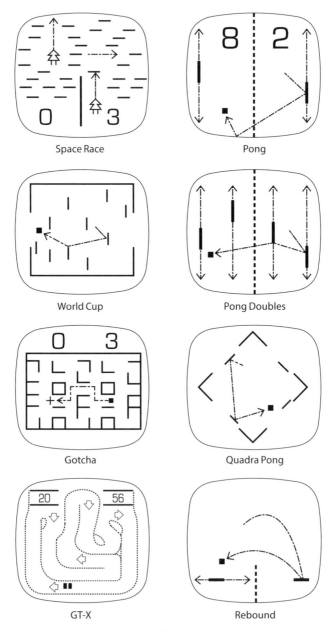

Space Race

Pong

World Cup

Pong Doubles

Gotcha

Quadra Pong

GT-X

Rebound

From *Game Machine*, no. 201 (1982)

Space Invaders' addition of movement and mythic imagination to the highly abstract concept of *Breakout* opened a completely new array of possibilities for the industry. The continuity of fundamental structure with the paddle-and-ball format of *Pong* remains visible, but the innovations of *Space Invaders* allowed that form to morph into something entirely new.

In *Space Invaders*, the blocks that had not moved in the earlier games now marched across—and down—the screen. Moreover, they were given the shape of invaders from space attacking the player. Behind the game lay the truly classic (almost outdated) mythic science fiction premise of a binary opposition between the earth and marauders from beyond. The abstract blocks of the earlier games are given an allegorical meaning that is all the more persuasive for its simplicity, and the playfield is transformed into a battlefield for an endless struggle against the invaders. Originally produced by the Japanese company Taito, the game was a great success both in Japan and in the United States. Unlike "capitalist" games like pinball, in which skill at controlling seemingly random outcomes was immediately converted to a numeric score, *Space Invaders* and its successors scored players on their destruction of invaders, and thus are arguably based on a "pre-capitalist cosmology." It is interesting to note that this game from Japan sought to "invade" foreign markets. In its introduction of novel movement along with ancient, mythic imagination, *Space Invaders* shares something of the character of the "techno-culture" that would follow.

There is one more important facet of *Space Invaders* that must not be overlooked. It is related to the fact that it is with this game that the industry adopted microprocessor CPUs in earnest. Most preceding games were constructed around transistor–transistor logic and black-and-white monitors. The CPU in *Space Invaders* accelerated access times significantly. The mass of aliens that moved across the screen did so smoothly, in digital color. Controls also grew increasingly more complex, from the original binary motion to movement in four and eventually eight directions. Though its popularity lasted only a year or two, *Space Invaders* awakened many to the vast potential of videogames.

Nothing made better use of that potential than *Xevious*, which was released by Namco in January 1983.

Xevious belongs to the genre of scrolling games, in which backgrounds change steadily as the game goes on. At the risk of over-simplifying, the game was a combination of action games that simulate a dogfight, such as *Space In-*

vaders, *Galaxian*, and *Galaga*, and driving simulation games with scrolling backgrounds like *Rally X* and *Pole Position*. The combination made the action of *Xevious* an unprecedentedly complicated scramble, combining aerial battle with hostile aircraft and attacks on ground targets in forests and enemy bases.

Beyond that, *Xevious* also managed to elevate the movement and mythic imagination introduced by *Space Invaders* to a higher level still. Even for a generation familiar since childhood with the gracefully moving images of animated films, the exquisite movement of the *Xevious* characters was shockingly fresh; even for a generation raised on space sagas and metaphysical science fiction emerging from the contemporary mythic imagination, *Xevious* was able to function as an interlocutor with significant depth of imagination. Much of the potential latent in the DNA of the videogame genotype since its inception with *Pong* seems to have been made manifest by *Xevious*. For this reason, *Xevious* enjoyed an unusually long stretch of popularity in the world of videogames, where products usually have a lifecycle measured in months.

Despite all this, explaining the charm of *Xevious* in a way that is easy to understand is a daunting task. Let's begin with the most basic level of this multilayered game: the way regular players enjoyed figuring it out even as they played it.

The biggest difference between *Space Invaders* and *Xevious* is the presence of a narrative component. *Space Invaders* is unbearably monotonous if played for any extended period of time, however high one's score rises. This is because games based on the mythic inside/outside dualism of earth/invaders from outer space lose the capacity to develop a narrative. Someone playing *Xevious*, however, can enter into an on-going "dialog" with the machine that might last for hours. This is due to the fact that, as the dialog develops, it also expands: the scrolling background spurs the player to imagine a profound narrative propelling the game.

The excitement of *Xevious*'s narrative manifests itself in two primary ways. One is the excitement of allusion. When passing through the third area of the Xevious army base, the player's Solvalou ship is threatened by a mass of spinning tiles called Bacuras. Even players with a passing knowledge of science fiction will recognize these as an allusion to the super-conscious monolith from Clarke and Kubrick's film *2001: A Space Odyssey*. Upon entering the seventh area of the base, players encounter a giant, beautiful "Nazca geoglyph," reminding them of the rich tradition of science fiction mythology about messages from space. The scrolling background taps a rich store of allusions from film, animation, and science fiction shared by both players and the game makers (led by Masanobu Endō who was in his early twenties). This connects the game to other, larger narratives, producing even deeper meaning for the player.

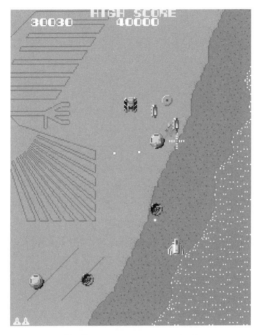

Xevious game screen shot
XEVIOUS® & ©BANDAI NAMCO Entertainment Inc.

However, there is another element of the game with an even greater capacity to evoke its latent narrative. The designers paid careful attention from the very beginning to constructing a grand science fiction tale that could encompass all the game's action and creating a narrative flow that would trigger waves of imagination as they designed the area map and wrote the game code.

The *Xevious* novel was filled with invented numerical symbols and words from the Xevi language. Up to its production, *Xevious* seemed very much like an animated film. One could say that it constructed an entire world. . . . Rather than a game scenario, the novel was closer to a pre-story. However, because it was circulated among and read by the development team, each and every enemy had a clearly delineated character, which improved the quality of the game's narrative.

From *The Making of Xevious*

This is how players who had not even heard of the novel (a digest of which appears in *Xevious: The Way to 10 Million Points*) could be drawn into the narrative by the images that scroll by, captured by the particular power of narrative to make one want to know what comes next.

Perhaps the part of *Xevious*'s backstory that generates the most narrative interest is the enemy's giant bases, the Andor Genesis motherships. The massive ships appear suddenly with a deep rumbling sound in areas four, nine, and fourteen. The only way to stop them is to destroy their central cores using the blasters normally reserved for ground targets. When they are destroyed, however, the Bragza—supposedly the Xevious army itself, having taken the form of a mass of black energy—ejects and flees to another mothership.

Mothership, Andor Genesis
XEVIOUS® & ©BANDAI NAMCO Entertainment Inc.

The narrative current that players sense in *Xevious* is in fact just such an indivisible and indestructible energy mass that runs through and controls the entire game. What players sense in the game is not the type of narrative one finds in a novel realized as a concrete object but rather the existence of a power that urges them to create a narrative themselves. Contact with this power leaves *Xevious* players with the strange impression that mythic powers of creation—mythopoetics—have been stimulated in them.

One additional thing that characterizes *Xevious* is the unusual movements of the enemy Xevious army. From the game's initial development stage, its designers looked to television animation as a model—its smoothness, its speed, and its humor, among other things—and attempted to express those things using computer animation. They were surprisingly successful.

Immediately after one presses the start button and the game begins, the Solvalou emerges from the forest and unmanned reconnaissance ships from the Xevious army, known as Toroids, appear directly in front of it. What surprises most first-time Xevious players is the smooth flying motion of these vessels. Instead of flying straight forward as expected, they suddenly roll to the side and change direction, as though taking evasive action, and then flee offscreen. Just as one gets used to this, one realizes that the enemy warships known as Torkan rotate their cockpits and flee immediately after launching their attacks. Zoshi, which means "death" in the Xevi language, are octopus-shaped ships that revolve as they approach. The flight patterns of these ships are so complex that at first it can be hard to predict which way they will go next.

Needless to say, the movements of the various ships in *Xevious* were built on advances in programming technique for such games as *Galaga* and *Bosconian*, but none refined these techniques to the exquisite heights of *Xevious*. This is partially due to its increase in the number of pattern rewrites used to express the movement of any given object. A good example of this is the pattern for the revolution of the manned, horseshoe crab–shaped Terrazi ships. The movement of this single enemy alone is represented using seven pattern rewrites.

The gameplay of *Xevious* is filled with surprising appearances and motion, disruptive explosions, rapid transformations, and humorous action. This catastrophic, disruptive, and surprising movement is overlaid on a narrative-producing energy that seems to flow uninterrupted throughout. For this reason, the energy that slowly builds to drive the narrative, to produce the myth, does not remain isolated, and the disruptive movement does not become simple noise. Instead, there is a synthesis of the mythic imagination and the cata-strophic, disruptive movement. It was that synthesis that gave *Xevious* a con-temporaneity that earlier games had been unable to achieve.

Were these the only things that *Xevious* had going for it, it would just be a well-made game machine. If players merely spent all their time destroying ene-my ships and ground targets in order to amass points, it would be reasonable to conclude that, even with the game's use of beautiful computer graphics that made possible smoother and quicker object movement than in any forerunner, not to mention the unprecedented level of profound mythic imagination un-derlying those graphics, *Xevious* was still nothing more than an aesthetically pleasing game. These achievements are, after all, not so very novel; certainly nothing that would warrant the claim of functioning as a type of psychothera-py. If the game only allowed the sort of play in which a player experienced fleet-ing joy, ease, and fatigue in the process of achieving a high score that represented his ability numerically, all within a paradise confined to the game world, *Xevious* would be just another of the long string of game machines produced by an industry that inculcated their players in a capitalist spirit based on the principle of competition.

If the game's players had been absorbed only in raising their high score, this would have been true. In fact, however, *Xevious* was used by a new generation of "game freaks" to discover a way of enjoying videogames that had few prece-dents. The "opponent" of these children, who had mastered the ability to steadi-ly increase their scores, ceased to be the Xevious army. Instead, they began a new battle, this time with the very computer program that made up the videog-ame. More specifically, their attention turned to the discovery of hidden char-acters and the various strange and rare phenomena that resulted from bugs in the software and data transfer within the hardware of the machine.

Children had learned early on that many hidden characters were built into the game. It is true that certain special events were programmed in, such as when a Sol Citadel (a memory tower for the Xevious army's hidden, under-ground computer) was revealed or a special flag popped up after a player bombed a specific point on the map. Game freaks turned their attention exclu-sively to the pleasure felt at the moment one of these hidden characters was discovered.

Before long word began to spread among children that even more secrets existed in the game. Players experienced events in the game that could not possibly have been meant to occur. Could it be that *Xevious*'s code, which had seemed almost divinely flawless, contained bugs (programming errors) that led to these sorts of strange phenomena? Or perhaps was it that particularly complicated attacks could overload the CPU in a way that caused these paranormal events to occur on-screen? Game freaks dedicated themselves to finding these black holes distributed throughout the program.

The strategy book *Xevious: The Way to 10 Million Points*, written by two of these young game freaks (Anzu Urusei and Naohiko Nakagane), reveals a number of such phenomena. According to *The Way*, the majority are the result of bugs in the code and timing errors that occur when data is transferred between the machine's CPUs. *Xevious* contained three CPUs: one for sound (*Xevious* was innovative in its background music as well; for more on that, please refer to Haruomi Hosono's *Videogame Music* [Alfa Records]), one called a Monster Allocation Unit (MAU) that stored pattern information for the different items, and one main CPU that ran the program as a whole. During gameplay, data was transferred between these CPUs at a dizzying rate. If timing was off even in the slightest, a variety of strange phenomena would occur, including:

1. After destroying the Argo of an Andor Genesis, the core is also destroyed and the game stops functioning, at which point the background goes black as though entering a tunnel. Eventually a previously unseen background appears, perhaps because of erroneous reading of the map data location.
2. A forest background appears in the spaces linking one area with another. Forest is the link between scrolling data, but it also places a heavy load on the CPU when it appears on the screen. This results in a number of strange forest-related phenomena.
3. In area fifteen's warp zone, the Solvalou warps back to area seven the moment it comes into contact with a missile from the Jara that approaches from behind. This unexpected warp occurs when the Solvalou is destroyed just as the command is reaching another CPU that the player has completed more than 70% of an area.

In addition to CPU-related issues, there are also a number of strange phenomena produced by bugs in the game's code. An example is the way in which, when Domograms emerge in circular formation, one Domogram might pass "beneath" the remains of another destroyed Domogram on the ground.

A number of the bugs discovered in the program were left there intentionally. (Given that manufacturers test-play new products for six months to a year before release, it is hard to imagine that they were not discovered.) The possibility of unexpected and unusual phenomena resulting from burdens placed on the hardware by the software was also left unaddressed. It is in precisely these two ways that *Xevious* broke new ground, creating possibilities for videogames that had not previously existed.

By cleverly leaving bugs unresolved, its designers gave *Xevious* a number of mysteries, a number of entrances to black holes. Even now, game freaks continue to transcend the capitalist pleasure of simply increasing their score and instead attempt to enter into a new "dialog" (also through battle) with the computer—or perhaps even with the consciousness of the universe itself. Through the visual data provided by the videogame, these children begin to develop an awareness, related to Gödel's incompleteness theorems, that were there no bugs at all, the computer program would be stuck, unable to function. They also come to possess a nomadic scientific awareness of the black hole entrances to infinity scattered throughout the universe. What remains unclear, however, is how the pleasures of playing with computer bugs will respond to that ever-changing chimera known as capitalism.

Works consulted:
Oppitz, Michael. "Shangri-la, le panneau de marque d'un flipper: Analyse sémiologique d'un mythe visuel." *l'Homme* 14 (3-4) (juillet-décembre 1974): 59-83.
Urusei, Anzu and Nakagane Naohiko. *Zebiusu: Issenman ten e no kaihō* [Xevious: The Way to Ten Million Points] (Tokyo: Game Freak, 1983).
"The Making of Xevious." LOGiN, May 1983.
Gēmu mashin [Game Machine] no.201, November 1982.

Appendix 3. The Origins of *Pokémon* by Satoshi Tajiri

The first time I met Shinichi Nakazawa in person was when he interviewed me for this book. For some reason, though, it did not feel like our first meeting. Why? In 1983, the appearance of *Xevious* (Namco) in arcades set off a feverish boom. I was just another kid crazy about games then, and I could not get enough. I started a hardcore fan magazine named *Game Freak* and published my friend's book, *Zebiusu: Issenman ten e no kaihō* [Xevious: The Way to Ten Million Points].

Around that time, Nakazawa published his essay "Gēmu furīku wa bagu to tawamureru [The Game Freaks Who Play with Bugs]," in which he clarified the myth-making powers of the game. My magazine was one of the works he cited.

His book *Pokketo no naka no yasei* [The Wildness in Your Pocket], which came out after that, once again cast a light from the world of words on me, a dyed-in-the-wool game freak. Why do video games enthrall so many people? Perhaps the people who create them also wrestle with this question unconsciously.

Nakazawa's analysis through language of the meaning of *Pokémon* and the structure of video games in general was invigorating. In a sense, this book performed the function of a bridge, linking the culture of games with other worlds. It provided us with a sense of fulfillment, as though we had discovered deep, deep forests in our games, gone through an adventure, and brought our spoils back to the contemporary world.

I was raised in a suburb in southwest Tokyo. When I was in elementary school in the 1970s, the roads were not even paved in the areas around the homes and apartment complexes where I was able to explore, and rice paddies, farmland, and woods still flanked the river I walked along on my way to school. But the places we played were gradually leveled, the small river was artificially straightened, and rows of homes were built. By my second year of middle school, my old play spots were gone. I did not feel any particular sense of nostalgia, but in the course of designing video games professionally, at some point I began to recall them. I remembered the *Space Invaders* boom that happened in my second year of middle school and changed my life. That had been the moment when a child obsessed with collecting insects became obsessed with videogames.

What did I do before I became obsessed with games? And why do I like games now? The ability to pull back memories and experiences such as these and use them to stimulate the imagination for future games can be said to have given birth to *Pokémon*. Of course, most of the game's development was concrete coding and design, and it was the integration of the ideas of team members who worked long hours dedicated to the same vision that completed the world of *Pokémon*.

If I were to get a little specific, I would identify one point in particular that I focused on as the game designer of *Pokémon*. Because programming, graphics, and sound effects are all done simultaneously as a game is developed, even if new ideas are hit upon later in the process, small things will be set aside and eventually forgotten. There are times, however, when inspiration that leads to significant improvements in the game strikes even after the process is underway. Particularly good ideas, if they impact the game as a whole, are worth implementing even if they are modest in size. Times like this test the leadership of the project head. Success, though, makes the game that much better and the sense of its world that much deeper.

One example of this occurred in the development of *Pokémon* around the autumn of 1995. It was already settled that when a player went into a wetland area of a field, a water-type Pokémon would appear. It was only after this that I thought of adding a fishing rod as a tool. If the player had a fishing rod when entering a wetland area, he could use it to catch a water-type Pokémon. Whether or not to do so would be left up to the player's discretion. Because the game's map had always had areas with water as an attribute, like swamps and the ocean, this development increased the quality of the game design. Adding the feature went smoothly, taking only one day to implement.

I should point out that the view of *Pokémon* today is different from that of *Pokémon* when Nakazawa wrote *Pokketo no naka no yasei* [The Wildness in Your Pocket].

At the time of Nakazawa's research, in March 1997, the world of Pokémon still retained its original form. The version for the Game Boy was the only one that existed. His timing was exquisite.

It was at precisely that moment that *Pokémon* experienced explosive growth in its popularity, particularly among primary school students. That month, sales of the software had just broken three million units. It was immediately before the *Pokémon* animated show began airing on the six TV Tokyo Network stations and twenty-four stations outside Tokyo on April 1. Even a cursory glance at this series would strongly suggest that Pikachu was the representative character of the game. This created the false impression that Pikachu was the key to *Pokémon*'s success. If one looked only at the Game Boy version, however, it was clear that Pikachu was only one of the 151 species of Pokémon. For these Game Boy players at least, their real dedication was to the specific Pokémon with them when they undertook their adventures.

However, from around this time, the reality of the story began to diverge depending on whether you had experienced *Pokémon* as a video game or as an animated show, or both.

Within the year, the game, animated show, trading cards, manga, and other related commodities had exploded in number and were spreading rapidly. The card-based game saw the introduction of particular "moves" for each Pokémon, but the concept of trading remained common throughout all versions of *Pokémon*.

In 1998 the game went on sale in the United States, Australia, Hong Kong, Taiwan, and Shanghai; it began to be recognized worldwide. *Pokémon* is slightly different depending on the country, region, and medium, but all its manifestations are spread out like simultaneous parallel worlds. Simply managing copyright over different media was an increasingly large operation, with more than one thousand cases of alleged infringement per month. (As of this writing, in September 2003, *Pokémon* software sales for the Game Boy and Game Boy Advance have exceeded one hundred and twenty million units. Including licensed products, the scale of the *Pokémon* business is roughly three trillion Japanese yen.)

When you look at the key elements that support the *Pokémon* world, they seem to increase forever. The raw feel of *The Wildness in Your Pocket* has even begun to feel like a thing of the past. But if one hones one's nerves, trying to recover those details, hints for returning to the original world come into view. When nature and science are brought into balance, things for which numbers matter are separated from things for which they do not, and the true form of *Pokémon* returns.

About the Author

Shinichi Nakazawa, born in Yamanashi in 1950, is an anthropologist and a philosopher who currently directs the Institut pour la Science Sauvage at Meiji University, Tokyo. Since his bestselling debut *Tibetto no Mōtsaruto* [Mozart in Tibet] (1983), based on his own experiences studying Buddhism in Tibet, he has written dozens of books exploring the relevance of premodern thought to contemporary life. His works include *Mori no barokku* [Forest of Baroque] (1992), *Āsu daibā* [Earth Diver] series (2005, 2012, 2017), and *Kumagusu no hoshi no jikan* [Kumagusu's Shining Moment] (2016).

（英文版）ポケモンの神話学　新版 ポケットの中の野生
The Lure of Pokémon: Video Games and the Savage Mind

2019 年 3 月 27 日　第 1 刷発行

著　者　中沢 新一
訳　者　テッド・マック
発行所　一般財団法人 出版文化産業振興財団
　　　　〒 101-0051 東京都千代田区神田神保町 3-12-3
　　　　電話　03-5211-7282（代）
　　　　ホームページ　http://www.jpic.or.jp/

印刷・製本所　大日本印刷株式会社

ISBN 978-4-86658-065-4